VITAMIN N

Vitamin N

The Essential Guide to a Nature-Rich Life

RICHARD LOUV

A companion handbook to
*Last Child in the Woods: Saving Our Children
from Nature-Deficit Disorder*
and
*The Nature Principle: Reconnecting
with Life in a Digital Age*

ALGONQUIN BOOKS OF CHAPEL HILL   2016

Published by
Algonquin Books of Chapel Hill
Post Office Box 2225
Chapel Hill, North Carolina 27515-2225

a division of
Workman Publishing
225 Varick Street
New York, New York 10014

Photo credits: © Jon Beard, pages 22, 174, 208; © Children &
Nature Network, page 262; © feverpitched/123RF, page 40;
© Heather Kuhlken Photography, pages 68, 138, 190; © Mandy
and Martin LeBlanc, pages 116, 206, 282; © Richard Louv, pages 12,
58, 256; © Janice Swaisgood, pages 20, 42, 90, 230, 260, 272;
© Elizabeth Wampler, Stephen J. Wampler Foundation, page 232.

Library of Congress Cataloging-in-Publication Data
Names: Louv, Richard, author.
Title: Vitamin N : the essential guide to a nature-rich life / Richard Louv.
Description: First edition. | Chapel Hill, North Carolina : Algonquin Books
    of Chapel Hill, 2016. | Includes bibliographical references.
Identifiers: LCCN 2015031470 | ISBN 9781616205782
Subjects: LCSH: Nature—Psychological aspects. | Nature study. |
    Outdoor recreation. | Family recreation.
Classification: LCC BF353.5.N37 L694 2016 | DDC 155.9/1—dc23
LC record available at http://lccn.loc.gov/2015031470

10 9 8 7 6 5 4 3 2 1
First Edition

To the thousands of people building
the new nature movement. And to my friend and colleague
Dean Stahl, who is one of them.

"What is life? It is the flash of a firefly in the night. It is the breath of a buffalo in the wintertime. It is the little shadow which runs across the grass and loses itself in the sunset."

—CROWFOOT, CHIEF OF THE SIKSIKA FIRST NATION, 1890

Contents

································

Introduction

IN SEARCH OF A NATURE-RICH LIFE

In 2009, Janet Ady of the U.S. Fish and Wildlife Service stood before a crowd of grassroots leaders gathered from across the nation by the Children & Nature Network. She held up an outsized pharmacy bottle. On the bottle was a physician's "prescription"—one that would be as appropriate for adults as it would be for children. The label read:

> DIRECTIONS: Use daily, outdoors in nature. Go on a nature walk, watch birds, and observe trees. Practice respectful outdoor behavior in solitude or take with friends and family. REFILLS: *Unlimited.* Expires: *Never.*

Here was a deceptively simple treatment for improving physical and mental health, for stimulating learning, creativity, and a sense of being fully alive; definitely not a panacea, but an appropriate elixir in the age of nature-deficit disorder.

The contents of the medicine bottle included a listing of National Wildlife Refuges by state, a guide to animal tracks, tips on how to experience nature without damaging it, information on planting native vegetation to help restore butterfly and bird migration routes, a protein bar, and other items—including paste-on tattoos depicting migratory birds. Later, Janet handed me the stage-prop medicine bottle.

In 2010, I was invited to give the plenary keynote to the annual national conference of the American Academy of Pediatrics (AAP), to several thousand pediatricians, pediatric nurse practitioners, and other professionals.

I reported on the growing body of scientific research on the benefits of nature experience for children and adults. The evidence indicates that experiences in the natural world may reduce the symptoms of Attention Deficit Hyperactivity Disorder, serve as a buffer to depression and anxiety, help prevent or reduce obesity and myopia, boost the immune system, and offer many other psychological and physical health benefits. Time spent in nature may also improve social bonding and reduce social violence, stimulate learning and creativity, strengthen the conservation ethic, and even help raise standardized test scores.

At the AAP conference, I held up Janet's medicine bottle and suggested to the doctors that they consider prescribing "vitamin N" — "N" for nature — as an antidote to nature-deficit disorder, which is not a medical diagnosis (though perhaps it should be), but a metaphor for the price paid, particularly by children, for our societal disconnect from the natural world.

Many of the pediatric professionals there that day were more than ready to start prescribing or recommending nature time for the families they served. Daphne Miller, MD, a general practitioner in Noe Valley, California, had already begun to write nature prescriptions as part of the burgeoning field of integrated medicine. "It's another tool in our toolbox." In Washington, DC, Robert Zarr, MD, now writes "park prescriptions." Zarr has even created an extensive database of Washington, DC's urban parks so that pediatricians know where to direct families.

For decades, people who worked directly with children and families in natural settings have been making the common sense case for nature's benefits. Today, they're bolstered by more science, and by a fast-growing new nature movement.

I should note that though most of the early studies were correlative, they pointed in the same direction—a rare occurrence for any emerging body of research. Many subsequent studies, some of them extensive and longitudinal, have underscored the earlier findings. Yes, we need more research, including studies that will show how nature experiences can best be applied. But as Howard Frumkin, dean of the School of Public Health at the University of Washington, has said, "We know enough to act."

Many public-health experts, psychologists, and psychiatrists are doing just that. So are policy makers, urban planners, and educators. A few years ago I wrote, half in jest, "Want your kids to get into Harvard? Tell 'em to go outside." In fact, nature-based education *is* spreading. Nature preschools and school gardens are multiplying. Even the National League of Cities has signed on.

Still, parents are the backbone of this movement. They don't have to wait for a physician to write a prescription or for a school board to change its policies. Parents can act now, as can anyone—single or married, urban or rural, of any age.

Last Child in the Woods and its sequel, *The Nature Principle*, which focused on adults, identified nature-deficit disorder as a societal diagnosis. *Vitamin N* takes the next step by serving as a companion handbook, offering a range of over five hundred practical actions that readers can apply in their everyday life and the life of their community. Parents will likely be the primary audience, but I hope *Vitamin N* will also be helpful to grandparents, aunts, uncles, teenagers, people without children of their own, and to teachers and other caring professionals whose work touches families every day.

As you use this book, I hope you'll keep the following in mind:

🌿 This book isn't just for kids.

Many of the actions in *Vitamin N* are focused on families with children, but all of us belong to some kind of family or circle of friends. Throughout the following pages you'll find activities for adults, too, and ones that can be adapted to the needs of most families, friends, and individuals.

🌿 Different abilities offer different opportunities.

I've offered some specific suggestions for children and adults with disabilities. Most of these actions can be adapted to the needs of people with special learning or physical requirements. And, as the section on the senses points out, physical or mental differences can sometimes foster exceptional abilities in the natural world.

🌿 Nearby urban nature is as essential as wilderness.

This book is for people who live in every kind of neighborhood: rural, suburban, or densely populated urban areas. It also recognizes that different cultures experience nature differently. And that's a good thing. This book also emphasizes that connecting with nature isn't only a spectator sport; it can also involve work, including conservation projects and the creation of new natural habitats in the most urban places.

🌿 Look for a balance between organized activities and those that encourage free, independent play and exploration.

Even though violent crime against children has decreased in recent years, safety is still a real concern in many neighborhoods. In the age of the twenty-four-hour news cycle, the fear of strangers remains a fact of life. So if kids are going to enjoy more experiences in nature, much of that time will require adult presence. However, please keep in mind that most of the supervised activities described in *Vitamin N* can be altered to provide more independent experiences.

Finally, *Vitamin N* should be an antidote to toxic stress, not the cause. This isn't a book of shoulds, but of possibilities. With that in mind, here's a suggestion: pick five or ten actions from these pages, try them, and come back for more if you wish. In the meantime, relax.

Take a break. Look at the clouds. Listen to the wind. Let the birds do the heavy lifting.

A Note to Readers

To learn more about research into the benefits to child and human development, please see the Children & Nature Network's research section at ChildrenandNature.org, as well as *Last Child in the Woods: Saving Our Children from Nature-Deficit Disorder* and *The Nature Principle: Reconnecting with Life in a Virtual Age.*

As with any approach to health, readers should consult with their physician or other health professional before making major changes in health regimens and lifestyle. Also, the legal discussions shared in these pages are not offered as legal advice.

No list of actions is ever complete. So please share your own creative ideas and help grow the movement at VitaminNforNature.com.

VITAMIN N

Part 1

· ·

The Gift
of Memory

*"If a child is to keep alive his inborn sense of wonder . . .
he [or she] needs the companionship of at least one adult
who can share it, rediscovering the joy, excitement, and
mystery of the world we live in."*

— RACHEL CARSON

YOU'RE NOT ALONE: STRENGTHENING THE BONDS OF FAMILY AND FRIENDSHIP

· ·

I s nature time absolutely necessary for a healthy, happy, fulfilling life? No. But for many children and adults it can make all the difference.

For some of us, experiencing the natural world is part of everyday life. We'd like to make more time and space for nature, learn about new paths or revive old ones. But for many folks, connecting with nature doesn't come naturally, even if we were privileged to have had that exposure when we were young. Electronic media, longer school hours, traffic, poor urban design, fear of strangers, the worry that we don't know enough to share nature; these are just some of the barriers. The purpose of this book is to show how those barriers can be overcome, beginning with simple actions at home.

Let's focus first on one of the most gratifying benefits of a nature-rich life: the building of stronger relationships within the family, among friends, and in the community.

What better way to enhance parent-child attachment than to go on a walk in the woods together, disengaging from distracting electronics, advertising, and peer pressure?

"Since the 1960s, child development research has yielded a wealth of information about the importance of the quality of parent-infant attachment as a powerful influence on a child's lifelong development," according to Martha Farrell Erickson, developmental psychologist and founding director of the Children, Youth & Family Consortium at the University of Minnesota. "Building gradually and slowly over the first year of a child's life, parent-infant attachment is a child's first close relationship and, to a large extent, a model for all relationships that follow."

As she writes in *Together in Nature: Shared Nature Experience as a Pathway to Strong Family Bonds*, "The natural world seems to invite and facilitate parent-child connection and sensitive interactions." Unplugging and taking a baby away from electronic distractions "creates an opportunity for what is called 'affective sharing'—oohing and aahing together over the sun shining through the leaves of a big tree . . . feeling a soft spring rain or a light winter snowfall on your face."

Start from Day One

🌿 **Give a baby the gift of nature.**
Introduce a newborn to the world outside. When our first son was born, I held him in my arms and walked to the window, and showed him his very first day. If the time and place are right, you can show your child the world in the beginning—the blue sky, gray clouds, the moon, the stars, the frost on the pane, the dawn.

🌿 **Use nature to reduce the stress of parenthood.**
Studies show that adults receive many of the same benefits as children from being outdoors: stress reduction, improvements in mental and physical health, and the ability to think more clearly and be more creative. Even before a child is born, nature time can be a healing time for parents.

🍃 **Calm an infant, through nature.**
Is a baby throwing a fit in a restaurant or other public setting? Take the baby outside, find a tree, and together explore the bark or leaves through sight and touch, while expressing excitement and surprise. In many cases this quickly calms a fussy child. Or an embarrassed, stressed-out parent.

🍃 **Explore the universe together.**
In your child's first months and years, and beyond, go to a park together, spread out a blanket, lie side by side for an hour or more; look up through moving leaves and branches at clouds or moon or stars. Bring water and milk. You may be there a long time.

🍃 **Get the right infant or child backpack carrier.**
To prepare for visiting nearby nature or hiking, parents will want to do some research before buying an infant or child carrier. One source for general information is the Consumer Reports guide to backpack carriers. REI provides information more specific to nature exploration. Both offer advice on appropriate sizes for different ages and weights, and information about safety and use.

🍃 **Get the right stroller, preferably an all-terrain model.**
As with backpack carriers, a stroller is a good device for exposing your baby or toddler to the sights, smells, and textures of the outdoors—especially when you stop along the way and talk about what you're experiencing. The first decision is whether you need a jogging stroller or an all-terrain stroller, which is best for hiking. Stroller-Envy.com shares advice about making the choice, as well as reviews and a buying guide.

🍃 **Use nature to reduce social isolation as a parent.**
Join one of the networks of parents who take their infants and toddlers into nature. "If you have an infant or toddler, consider organizing a neighborhood stroller group that meets for weekly nature walks," suggests the National Audubon Society. Existing

networks include the Yahoo group Nature Strollers (Groups. Yahoo.com), which organizes walking and hiking groups for families with babies, toddlers, and young children. ToddlerTrails .com provides a directory linking moms, dads, and grandparents to fun "toddler/family" friendly activities, places, and things to do in Orange County, California, and surrounding cities. If such a network doesn't exist in your region, band together with other parents and start one.

Take the "Hike it Baby" challenge.

Feel competitive? Hike it Baby 30 (www.hikeitbaby.com) sponsors a national quarterly campaign to encourage families to get outside for a walk or hike for a minimum of thirty minutes a day for at least half of the month. The minutes can be completed by mom, dad, aunt, uncle, grandparent, nanny, or anyone who wants to get outside with a baby.

Begin to build a nature vocabulary.

On a nature walk with your toddler, point out objects or landscape features. This will help anchor the words to what is seen, felt, or heard, according to the National Association for the Education of Young Children: "By providing real objects, we help infants associate words with the concrete objects they represent."

When walking with toddlers, go slow and be ready for sudden stops.

Let them lead the way. Encourage them to stop to turn over rocks, touch moss, toss pebbles into a puddle or pond, and, when they can, climb on and over rocks and fallen trees. Whatever the environment, which you assess for any unreasonable hazards, the toddler can set the pace—stimulating confidence, agility, problem solving, creativity, and a sense of wonder.

Watch your child become fascinated with a blade of grass, a pebble, the way the clouds move.

Don't interrupt.

SIMPLE WAYS TO EXPAND TIME AND SPACE FOR KIDS AND ADULTS

Many of us hunger for unscheduled free time in nature, with good reason. Research shows that when children play in natural spaces, they're far more likely to invent their own games than in more structured settings—a key factor in becoming self-directed and inventive as children and later in life. In fact, creativity and learning throughout life can be stimulated by more time in nature. But here's the paradox. To make time for unorganized time in nature, a busy family is probably going to have to organize a lot of it. Doing that with a sense of proportion and humor helps.

🍃 **Put nature on the calendar.**

If you plan the family's sports commitments and vacations in advance, do the same for time spent in nature. Try skipping organized sports for a season and use that time to get outside. That suggestion won't work for everyone, but for busy families, taking time for nature requires *taking* time—and putting it on the calendar.

🍃 **Practice "friluftsliv."**

"Friluftsliv" is a Norwegian term, introduced in 1859, that roughly translates as "free air life." It's a general lifestyle idea that promotes outdoor activity as good for all aspects of human health. The protocol is pretty straightforward—just be outside as much as possible. Work it into your schedule by committing to being in nature for a minimum amount of time every day, or a certain number of days a month.

🍃 **Think of nature time as enrichment time.**

Leisure is good. Of course! Play is essential. But our culture tends to dismiss independent play, leisure, and nature time as nonessential nice-to-haves. But in terms of child development, or human development at any age, nature time is as important as activities we now consider educational or developmental enrichment.

🍃 **Turn your commute time into a nature safari.**
If you're stuck in traffic, entertain yourself and your kids by keeping an eye out for plants, animals, or other natural curiosities on the side of the road. If you see something really intriguing, pull over and take a look. "We've pulled over more times than I can count because one of us spotted something worth watching. Cool cloud formations, gorgeous sunsets and make-you-smile rainbows. And the birds — oh, the birds — they never disappoint!" says one mother.

🍃 **Take a First Day Hike.**
New to hiking? No problem. State parks, many of them in urban areas or close by, offer hundreds of guided First Day Hikes (referring to the first day of January), to individuals and families with kids eight years old or older. For more information about the First Day Hike program, go to AmericanHiking.org.

🍃 **Walk this way.**
On their first hike, younger children can enjoy playing a game called "walk this way" — imitating different animals along the way. Bring toys and props that will make it more fun, like hats and fake swords. Walkie-talkies are also a big hit. Encourage kids to take turns as "hike leader," walking in front and setting the pace. To help kids pay attention during longer hikes, play find ten critters — which means discovering footprints or other signs of an animal passing through. Recommended book: *The Down and Dirty Guide to Camping with Kids.*

🍃 **Go on a moon walk.**
Take a family walk when the moon is full. Cindy Ross is a longtime devotee of full-moon walks. "We've walked by balmy summer moons in T-shirts, with katydids singing and lightning bugs flashing in a multi-sensory display." But the best moon walks, she says, are under the winter moons. "I started out going on full moon walks for myself . . . but I also did it for my children, so they would

grow up to realize there is much magic in the natural world and most of it is free." Bring a flashlight, of course, but it's important to turn it off sometimes and let your senses emerge and adjust. Listen for animal sounds (a whole new crew is out at night), watch for the silhouettes of owls and bats looking for prey, and keep your eye out for life that glows, including glow worms and fungus on trees.

Set a star date.

If your family is lucky enough to live where the stars are visible, stargaze in the evening or very early morning. In the yard, from a balcony, or out beyond the city lights, take a blanket, binoculars, or small telescope, and stargaze together. With your kids, locate a few key constellations and orient to those. Air and light pollution prevent two-thirds of the U.S. population and more than half of Europe's population from seeing the Milky Way with the naked eye. Schools, sky-watcher groups, amateur meteorologists, and even star charts in our smartphones can help. Good resources include For Spacious Skies, a sky-awareness program, and Dark Sky Initiative, which works to preserve and protect the nighttime environment.

Lose the cell phone; get a better connection.

Tech isn't the enemy, but it can certainly be a barrier. Vow to leave your cell phone in your pocket, ringer off, as well as all the beeps, tweets, and repeats, so you're more present to your child. Limit access to texting, computers, and TV part of the day or week. For example, schedule Saturday as a "Smartphone and iPad-Free Outdoor Play Day" for the kids and the parents as well (more about that later).

Play hooky.

That's right. Hooky, preferably with the teacher's permission. In his book, *Home Grown: Adventures in Parenting off the Beaten Path*, Ben Hewitt suggests that parents of school-aged children "take them out of school for a day." And take the day off work yourself. He suggests unplugging all screens at home and, for at least part of the day, heading for the woods, a park, the middle of a hayfield, with no agenda.

GIVE THE GIFTS OF NATURE AND CREATE NEW FAMILY AND FRIENDSHIP RITUALS

This holiday season, give a partridge in a pear tree. If you can't find a partridge or a pear tree, here are a few suggestions for natural gifts for any occasion. Some of these can inspire direct experience. Others can *be* the experience. All of them can last for decades.

🍃 **Make an outdoor coupon book.**
Give your child, other family member, or friend an envelope with several coupons for day hikes, fishing trips, tree climbing, stargazing, wild watching, a mound of dirt (cheaper than a video game), or any of the gifts below. These coupons can be redeemed during the holidays or throughout the year.

🍃 **Hold a holiday or family celebration outdoors.**
Bring your next birthday, anniversary, or family reunion into nature. Kathy Ambrosini, an environmental educator in New York, suggests this holiday approach: "Change it up this Thanksgiving! Invite family to come early for a pre-feast walk. Those who stay overnight can join you for a walk at a neighborhood preserve in the morning." Do it twice, and make it a new family tradition. Need an alternative site? Some nature centers offer indoor and outdoor spaces for special events.

🍃 **Create a gardening gift basket.**
Assemble seeds for native plants, trowels, kneepads, and other gardening tools, and plant a traditional vegetable or flower garden. Or, go native. Include a guide to local native plants and animals (or

download and assemble your own guide from online resources. Add a journal to record the progress of the garden, and, if you go native, to record the native insects and other critters that show up to rebuild the food web.

🍂 **Put together a family G.O. Bag.**

Stuff a duffel bag with daypacks, a compass, binoculars, nature guides, and maybe a topo-map of your bioregion. Add granola bars, hats, gloves, fleece vests, sunglasses, collapsible hiking poles, some old hiking shoes or other comfortable footwear, and water bottles. Wrap your G.O. Bag. Stash it in your car trunk. Now your family can Go Outside on a moment's notice.

🍂 **Create natural decorations for holidays and birthday.**

Create holiday ornaments or cards from sticks, rocks, and leaves. For a wreath, bend a wire hanger into a circle. As suggested in *The Kids' Outdoor Adventure Book*, gather evergreen branches and wrap them around the hanger, securing with twine. Collect other natural materials from the yard or nearby nature to decorate it. Add some berries and a bow. Now take a bow.

🍂 **Give a book that will inspire an outdoor adventure.**

Most of us can recall our favorite childhood books: picture books, books for early and middle readers, and for young adults. As gift books, the ones that parents and other family members loved when they were children will have special meaning for kids. The books most likely to inspire children to head outdoors aren't environmental sermons (plenty of time for those later), but about adventure and wonder. Such inspirational titles include *Island of the Blue Dolphins, Julie of the Wolves, Tom Sawyer, The Jungle Book*, and *The Curious Garden*. And don't forget adult family members and friends; inspire them with Robert Michael Pyle's *The Thunder Tree*, Jon Young's *What the Robin Knows*, Edward Abbey's *Desert Solitaire*, and Rachel Carson's *The Sense of Wonder*.

🍃 Make the "green hour" a new family tradition.

The National Wildlife Federation recommends that parents give their kids a daily green hour for unstructured play and interaction with the natural world. Can't spare a green hour? Fifteen minutes is a good start. "Imagine a map with your home in the center. Draw ever-widening circles around it, each representing a successively older child's realm of experience," NWF suggests. "Whenever possible, encourage some independent exploration as your child develops new skills and greater confidence."

🍃 Take a vacation or staycation at a state or national park.

Participate in one of the family or group outing programs offered by local and state parks, such as Connecticut's Great Park Pursuit. Some programs offer fishing lessons, hiking events, and geocaching treasure hunts. Around the country, national and state parks may seem overcrowded, but that crush is mainly on the roads. The vast number of visitors to national and state parks never venture farther than a few yards from their cars.

🍃 Purchase a family park pass.

National parks, national monuments, and some refuges and regional parks exist in urban as well as wilderness areas. Many parks charge for admission, but as *Forbes* magazine points out, they aren't a bad deal when compared to other forms of recreation: "Going to a movie for a family of four can cost around $80. Bowling for four for two hours on a Saturday can cost around $90, not including food." In comparison, an unlimited annual family pass to the national parks costs $80; it's free for members of the military and those with permanent disabilities. (Beginning in September 2015, all fourth graders in the United States—and their families—became eligible for a free annual pass to the national parks and other federal natural lands.)

🍃 Plant a family or friendship tree, or adopt one.

Adopt or plant a tree to help mark important family occasions—a holiday, a birth, death, or marriage. The Arbor Day Foundation has information about tree-planting opportunities. Susan J. Tweit, plant biologist and author of *Walking Nature Home*, offers this suggestion: "Get to know a tree or shrub in your neighborhood intimately by observing it over the course of a growing season. Every week, check your adopted tree or shrub and note any changes." The Take a Child Outside Week campaign suggests taking pictures of your live family tree in its first snow or after a big windstorm. Make bark rubbings using crayons and paper. Make a digital adoption notebook with photos, videos, and observations. Plant its seeds. If the tree dies, save some leaves or branches as remembrances. "If you share your observations, you'll be giving scientists useful data to track climate change," she says. To get started, visit Project Budburst or Nature's Notebook, and set up an account for your adopted tree or shrub.

🍃 Build memories, but don't expect immediate results.

Especially for older children and teenagers, shared outdoor experiences encourage indirect communication—rather than the kind of in-your-face parental quizzes they dread. Even if the payoff isn't immediately visible, wait for it. When reminiscing with their families about childhood memories, grown children seldom mention the best day they spent watching TV or playing a video game. Among the memories they do recall, if they're lucky enough to have had such experiences with their families, are outdoor adventures—even if they complained loudly about such outings at the time.

🍃 Give the gift of radical amazement.

The great teacher Abraham Joshua Heschel once wrote that our goal should be to live life in radical amazement. Birthdays and holidays are an especially good time to remind ourselves that this is so.

As Heschel advised, take nothing for granted: "Everything is phenomenal; everything is incredible; never treat life casually. To be spiritual is to be amazed." Along with sharing time, radical amazement is the best present you can offer, best delivered by example. And you don't even have to wrap it.

MAKE ROOM FOR INDEPENDENT PLAY AND SOLITUDE

While it's essential to put nature on the calendar, parents and other guardians also need to know when to unschedule. Tamra Willis, associate professor in the College of Education at Mary Baldwin College in Staunton, Virginia, suggests parents be aware of the tension between independent and structured play. But rather than feeling compelled to choose between guided or independent play, consider play a spectrum of activities. There's a time to guide. There's a time to share the experience together. There's a time to step back. And there's a time for solitude.

🌿 **Recognize that boredom isn't necessarily a negative.**
Especially during summer, parents hear the moaning complaint: "I'm borrrred." Boredom is fear's dull cousin. Passive, full of excuses, it can keep children from nature—or drive them to it. Many of us recall how carefully planned activities paled in comparison to more spontaneous experiences, and that boredom often pushed us to create our own stories, which we tell to this day.

🌿 **Be the guide on the side.**
"Parents should encourage children to explore by asking questions and helping them find answers," says Willis. "There are other times when a parent or teacher should be the 'guide on the side.'" Environmental educator Joe Baust agrees and suggests the next step on the spectrum: "Don't be the sage on the stage, set the stage"—a setting for more independent play, with less or no adult supervision or instruction.

Inspire curiosity by example, and accept that you don't have to know everything.

At times, the parent should lead the way, and actively teach, but other times parents should encourage the child to be the guide—the outdoor leader of adults or other kids. Step back. You don't have to be a Master Naturalist to know which way the wind blows. Sometimes just introducing a child to the wind is magic enough. You may even discover that you haven't listened—really listened—to the wind in years. Excitement is contagious. Be a new learner, along with your child—be open to new things. Encourage questions to which you don't know the answer: "I don't know! Let's find out together." Recommended book: *The Nature Connection: An Outdoor Workbook for Kids, Families, and Classrooms.*

To encourage independent play, meet up with other families and friends.

This may seem counterintuitive, but one way that parents can encourage kids to play in unstructured ways is to join other families outdoors. Doing so makes it easier for parents to feel comfortable standing back and letting the kids play on their own. Children are more likely to forget the electronics waiting at home and join with other kids in spontaneous play.

Start or Join a Family Nature Club

· ·

None of us raises our children by ourselves. Parents need the help of other family members—their own parents and grandparents, for example—and we need the companionship of other families. The gap between children and the rest of the natural world has widened in the recent decade. Therefore, many young parents today had little experience with nature when they were kids.

Here's a way to create a community of support for parents and children: Join an existing family nature club, or form a new one. It's a great way to create a community of support for families. This same concept can be adopted by teens or adults without children of their own, in the form of *friendship* nature clubs.

"Our first son, Owen, who was born prematurely, had his first adventure outside of the neonatal intensive care unit on a hike in San Diego's Mission Trails Regional Park," says Janice Swaisgood, a mother of two and former teacher. "Now and then we invited friends to join us on our hikes and camping trips, mostly new families that I had met through a breast-feeding support group."

But Janice and her husband, Ron, still found it difficult to find the time for nature excursions, or to schedule trips with other families.

Then, four years ago, they read about parents in Roanoke, Virginia, who had launched a free outdoor adventure club for families, mapping out hikes, publishing a monthly schedule of outdoor activities on their website, and inviting other families to join them.

The unofficial members of this new club agreed to meet up at the park, or garden together, or do conservation projects together, or hike in nearby wilderness, rain or shine, with two, five, or ten families at a time.

One rule was absolute: parents or guardians were required to stay with their children at all times, not only for safety, but to make sure that children and parents, and sometimes grandparents, were making memories together. This wasn't a drop-off daycare service.

The idea was contagious. Janice and Ron started their own family nature club, which they named Family Adventures in Nature (FAN).

Eight volunteer leaders now organize the outings weekly, biweekly, or monthly. "We've been known to fill a campground within hours of posting a scheduled campout," says Janice. Some families like strenuous regional hikes; others prefer closer-to-home adventures. These families continued as members of FAN, but created smaller groups within it. Janice calls them Nearby Nature Clubs. Today, more than fifteen hundred families belong to San Diego's FAN club. "We've had two or three members move to other parts of the country and start their own clubs where they live."

Here are some of the benefits of nature clubs for families.

- They break down key barriers, including fear of strangers. There's perceived safety in numbers.

- They can be created in any neighborhood—whether inner-city, suburban, or rural—and in any economic setting.

- They can be joined or created by any family—single parents, extended families, friends who feel like families.

- Motivation: It's much more likely you and your family are going to show up at a park on Saturday morning if you know there's another family waiting for you.

- Shared knowledge: Many parents want to give their kids the gifts of nature, but they don't feel they know enough about nature to do so.

- Friendship: Parents and kids make new friends, and widen their social network.

- Importantly, there is no need to wait for funding. Families can do this themselves and do it now.

Chiara D'Amore, who recently received her doctorate in Sustainability Education from Prescott College, wrote her dissertation about the remarkable impact of family nature clubs, particularly for those families who face extra challenges in their lives. Here are a few voices from the parents she interviewed:

"My family has experienced many unforeseen set-backs this year. If it had not been for learning what I have in the nature play group about the benefits of free outdoor exploration and play I do not think we would have made it through."

"My youngest son has autism and he seems to do better on days that we are outside exploring nature. He becomes focused, he listens . . . Also I love how excited both my children get . . . When we camp they learn to work together to accomplish a task. They don't even realize they are learning."

"As a foster father, I don't have the same emotional attachment to the children in our care as my wife does. Participating in the family nature club gives me a chance to bond with them in ways I hope they remember for the rest of their lives."

Today, there are more than two hundred family nature clubs in North America, many of them with hundreds of member families. More family nature clubs are on the way, via Children & Nature Network (C&NN) partner campaigns from the American Zoo Association, Canadian Wildlife Federation, and the National League of Cities.

What if there were thousands of nature clubs for families? We'd be well on our way to true cultural change.

To see a list of existing nature clubs for families that you might join, go to the C&NN website at childrenandnature.org. Or better yet, start your own. Download a free C&NN Nature Clubs for Families Tool Kit.

Other Voices

"Bend some rules if necessary. Dinnertime or bedtime can be made into a moveable feast to facilitate some outdoor game that has just transcended time."　　*—Bernard Joyce, Ballyvary, Ireland*

"We get together with a tribe of homeschoolers for regular campouts, five to seven days at a time. We aim for several trips a year. We set up at a group site or a cluster of sites. Parents set up kitchens together and tents around the perimeter. Kids are then set free. We feed, water and sunscreen them as needed (the youngest are appropriately supervised). The older kids have freedom to explore rocks, forests, deserts, caves, beaches, depending on where we are. Their time is theirs. They band together in multi-age groups and have a splendid time. It's the best thing we do."　　*—Stephanie Funke Crary, Arizona*

"We let our eighteen-month-old get into most anything outside. He's tasted dirt, bark, rocks, flowers. He's smelled a decaying deer carcass we found on a hike. Unless he is headed for an overtly dangerous situation (common sense prevails here), we let him do whatever he wants in the yard and on hikes and camping trips. He figures out ways to entertain himself much faster outside than he does in a room full of toys. For us, Utah's mountains are a natural playground and learning laboratory."　　*—Jonny Griffith, Utah*

"We have a rule. When out camping you can get as dirty as you want as long as you are not eating or in the tent."
—Heather Monchak Nichols, St. Louis, Missouri

"On Father's Day I am going to start it as I have all the rest, with a call to my dad saying thanks for working so hard and still finding the commitment to get us outside and active. Then I'm going to take my two-year-old son on a hike."

—Ray Rivera, Denver, Colorado

Part 2

. . . .

Ways of Knowing the World

"Every child should have mud pies, grasshoppers, water bugs, tadpoles, frogs, mud turtles, elderberries, wild strawberries, acorns, chestnuts, trees to climb, brooks to wade in, water lilies, woodchucks, bats, bees, butterflies, various animals to pet, hay fields, pine cones, rocks to roll, sand, snakes, huckleberries and hornets; and any child who has been deprived of these has been deprived of the best part of his education."

— LUTHER BURBANK

"There is a sixth sense . . . that is the sense of wonder."

— D. H. LAWRENCE

THE HYBRID MIND

. . . .

Optimistic researchers suggest that digital technology is creating the smartest generation yet, freed from limitations of geography, weather, and distance — those pesky inconveniences of the physical world. Other people, including many educators, are skeptical, if not hostile to technology.

Here's a third possibility: the Hybrid Mind. As I wrote in *The Nature Principle*, the Hybrid Mind represents the ultimate multitasking, which is to use computers to maximize our ability to process intellectual data, and natural environments to ignite our senses and accelerate our ability to learn and feel.

I once met a man who trained young people to become cruise ship pilots. He said he encountered two kinds of students. One kind grew up mainly indoors, spending hours playing video games and working on computers. These students were quick to learn the ship's electronics, a useful talent, the instructor explained. The other kind of student grew up spending a lot of time outdoors, often in nature. They, too, had a necessary talent. "They actually know where the ship is."

He wasn't being cute. To him, the ultimate student would be one with both sets of abilities, abilities that come from both virtual and natural experience. "We need people who have both ways of knowing the world," he added.

Recent studies of the human senses—including a cluster of spatial senses—back up that statement. Scientists who study human perception no longer assume we have only five senses: taste, touch, smell, sight, and hearing. The number now ranges from a conservative ten to as many as thirty human senses, including proprioception (awareness of our body's position in space), echolocation, and a more acute sense of smell.

Each is a doorway into learning—to *knowing*.

In the following pages, I share some activities that will help parents heighten their children's and their own sensory awareness through experiences in nature, with or without the help of technology.

COUNTERACT SENSORY DYSFUNCTION

Angela Hanscom, a pediatric occupational therapist, author of *Balanced & Barefoot*, and creator of the TimberNook camps, asks, "Why can't our kids sit still?"

She views nature as "the ultimate sensory experience for all children and a necessary form of prevention for sensory dysfunction. The more we restrict children's movement and separate children from nature, the more sensory disorganization we see." Many teachers report that children are frequently falling out of their seats in school, running into walls, and tripping over their own feet, and they are unable to pay attention. Some of this behavior, Hanscom argues, is related to sensory dysfunction. She recommends the following simple nature activities for building sensory awareness:

🍃 Play in mud puddles.

As kids maneuver through the mud, they test their balance, visual scanning skills, and engage their tactile (touch) senses as they search for a frog.

● **Climb trees, listen to the birds.**

Scaling a tree, testing branches, teaches safety skills. And the tree offers a natural touch experience and the vestibular (balance) sense. Encouraging kids to listen to and identify bird sounds helps them develop spatial awareness and stimulates their hearing and sight.

● **Roll down grassy hills; go sledding.**

Rolling down hills provides needed deep pressure to muscles and ligaments, which improves balance and the proprioceptive sense in the joints and muscles. "This sense is fundamental to helping children accurately regulate how much force to use when playing games like tag, or using a pencil without breaking the lead, or holding a baby chick without squeezing too hard," according to Hanscom. "If you're lucky enough to have snow, sledding is a great sensory activity, especially if you frequently change positions on the sled."

● **Walk or run in natural environments.**

Running through the woods improves balance and teaches children to navigate their environment. When kids walk on logs outdoors, other senses are activated as well: sensations of moist versus dry, crunchy versus soft, noisy versus quiet, and changes in temperature.

● **Build forts, dens, and tree houses.**

These activities help children with problem solving, creativity, and planning. They increase the amount of sensory input that they experience, while igniting their imaginations.

HIDDEN SUPERPOWERS

Spending more time outdoors can activate or tune underused senses, including ones that many of us don't realize we have. One way parents can encourage kids to connect with nature, and themselves, is to explore these human supersenses, or superpowers, which can be developed outdoors. In some cases, one sense can be enhanced when another sense is compromised. For example, little Teddy Roosevelt, with his poor eyesight as a child, learned to imitate hundreds of birdcalls, and continued to do so as an adult (which may make him the first U.S. president to tweet). Here are some activities that extend Hanscom's recommendations.

🌿 **Rotate the senses.**
Don't fixate; vary sensory awareness. "If you pay rapt attention to one thing, it will dull your senses ('highway hypnosis')," according to Princeton University's Outdoor Action initiative. "Flash back and forth through your various senses, vision, hearing, smell, touch, and taste."

🌿 **Help a child get close to the earth: go on a belly hike.**
To take a micro-hike, kids inch along on their bellies, covering just a few feet, and view "such natural wonders as grass blades bent by rainbow dewdrops, colorful beetles sprinkled with flower pollen, and powerful-jawed eight-eyed spiders," suggests Joseph Cornell in *Sharing Nature with Children*. He adds, "Because young children are particularly fond of tiny objects, their interest absorption in the world of the forest-in-miniature will amaze you."

🌿 **Encourage barefoot explorers.**
In 2010, the *Guardian* reported "a growing belief among experts that when it comes to children's footwear, the best shoe may be no shoe at all." Some podiatrists contend that walking barefoot develops foot muscles, ligaments, arch strengh, and (where sharp objects aren't present) can actually be safer than wearing shoes, especially flip-flops. One reason is that going barefoot improves

proprioception — awareness of where we are in relation to the space around us. Barefoot walkers are more likely to look down, to take care where they step, are less likely to fall. Walking barefoot enhances awareness of texture and terrain. Some proponents offer, well, cosmic reasons for going barefoot, but anyone who has spread their toes in cool grass knows the best rationale. Recommended books: *Barefoot Walking* and *Whole Body Barefoot.*

Find your inner bloodhound.

Researchers at the University of California, Berkeley, wondered if human beings could follow a scent trail with their ears and eyes covered. The researchers found that not only are humans capable of scent tracking, but they intuitively mimic the tracking pattern of other mammals that make their livings with their nose. Simply wetting one's nose can stimulate the sense of smell. Here's another way. Walk through the woods or a field, or along a creek, and have your kids report what they smell — then ask them to list and describe these smells in a nature journal. Audubon suggests making "sniffer cups." "Give each child a small paper or plastic cup . . . Have the kids select natural objects such as pine needles, bark, dirt, and flowers." Smell the difference. Then mix them up in the cup with a stick or spoon to create a new smell.

Learn to use a snake tongue, deer ears, or owl eyes.

Heather Stephenson, in an essay titled, "How to Keep Young Hikers Happy," suggests having kids use their "snake tongues" "to try tasting the air, seeing which way the wind is blowing, and sensing the temperature." She describes an exercise called "Deer Ears and Owl Eyes," a technique she learned from the Appalachian Mountain Club: "Cup your hands around your ears to listen to what's in front of you, or cup them backward to hear what's behind you better, imitating the way deer shift their ears to hear. Notice all the sounds that are usually covered by hikers' chatter. Then look with 'owl eyes,' forming binoculars with . . . your hands to imitate owls' fixed, forward-facing eyes, and turning all around."

Take the trail less seen.

Blindfold kids and adults and have them follow a rope through varied terrain in which they can smell, hear, and feel things. Have them retrace their steps without the blindfold to see how much more they notice. Or, while on a walk, instruct kids to stop and close their eyes. Ask them questions about their environment: "What direction are the clouds moving?" and "Were there any birds in the tree we just passed?" Recommended books: *Sharing Nature with Children* and *Coyote's Guide to Connecting with Nature*.

Practice focused hearing to "see" with your ears.

On a family outing, use focused hearing. Because our ears are on the sides of our heads, and because we can't move our ears as many other animals can, humans have good peripheral hearing but poor focused hearing. "But we can increase our hearing by tenfold by cupping our hands, thumbs up, behind our ears, with the elbows out," writes Rick Curtis, of Princeton University's Outdoor Action. "This creates a parabolic reflector, which gathers the sound in to our ears."

Be a Batman or a Batwoman.

Echolocation is the system bats use to navigate in the dark. In 2009, researchers at Madrid's University of Alcalá de Henares showed how people, like bats, could identify objects without needing to see them, through the echoes of human tongue clicks. According to the lead researcher, echoes are also perceived through vibrations in the ears and bones. This refined sense is learned through trial and error by some blind people and even sighted individuals.

A Real-Life Batman

·······································

The most famous example of someone who has learned to use eco-location is Daniel Kish, who lost his vision when he was a year old. As an adult, Kish has climbed mountains, ridden bikes, and lived alone in the wilderness, *Smithsonian* magazine reports. Kish, who has been dubbed "a 'real-life Batman,' is able to perform these tasks because of his uncanny ability to 'see' by echolocation," according to *Smithsonian*. Learn more from Kish's nonprofit World Access for the Blind.

In the meantime, help your kids test their own ability. In a natural setting—they, and you—listen carefully for a half hour, or longer, and create a mental map of what the ears "see."

It's all about hearing a world that exists beyond what we normally mistake for silence or darkness.

EXTRA WAYS TO DEVELOP
EXTRA-VISION

Parents can help kids see a whole world beyond the screen—and in the process, see it themselves. Ecolocation is one alternative way to "see" the world, but more direct and familiar techniques are available.

🌿 **Use pinpoint vision to notice the miraculous in the smallest places and patterns.**

In the era of sixty-inch TV screens, we're so accustomed to taking in spectacular panoramas that when we actually get outdoors, we can miss the trees for the forest. "I found the splendor of nature in the 'forgotten' wilderness," wrote Tom Brown, Jr., author of a best-selling series of handbooks on the outdoors. Kids and adults can discover that wilderness in the pattern of lichen on the side of a rock, the texture of bark, the insects and smallest lizards that hide in the crevices of the forgotten wilderness, which exists in the nearby nature of our yards as well as in the great parks. The trick is to look closely, and *notice.*

🍃 **Use wide-angle or "splatter" vision for the big picture, and to detect movement.**

Pinpoint vision is useful, but it can be overused in everyday life. More and more of our day is spent using a more-limiting form of pinpoint vision, locked in on, say, the screen of a computer or a smartphone. Wild animals spend most of their time using wide-angle vision. They see the big picture. So for humans, wide-angle or splatter vision is more sensitive to movement than pinpoint vision. Brown suggests looking toward the horizon and allowing your vision to spread out. "Instead of focusing on a single object, allow the eyes to soften and take in everything in a wide half-sphere." Here's another exercise to experience wide-angle vision: spread your arms as far as possible to each side and look straight ahead. "Then, wiggling your fingers, bring your hands gradually forward until you detect the first flicker of movement out of the corners of your eyes."

🍃 **Practice wide-angle vision at night.**

Because peripheral vision is more sensitive to low levels of light, using wide-angle vision at night can be more effective than using a flashlight, which forces pinpoint vision. Instead, use your wide-angle vision to look for patterns. For example, at night, a wind will blow leaves and grass in a rhythm. If you notice anything moving contrary to that rhythm, then focus in with your pinpoint vision.

🍃 **Practice automatic vision.**

As we scan, when we see something moving, we can "take a picture" of it, hold it in our minds, then continue to scan. When our eyes move across the landscape again, they tend to focus on the same spots. "The blind spots (dead air space) are the ones you miss. Over time the number of automatic snapshots decreases until you only see a few out of the whole scene," says Outdoor Action's Rick Curtis. "Eventually you really don't see it at all. You must consciously fight dead air space all the time. Each time you look at a scene again, look at it as something new."

🍃 **Look between the spaces.**

"Also, don't just look at solid objects (e.g., a tree); look through the spaces of the tree, between the branches," Curtis adds. "There may be a deer behind that tree that you will see if you look through it rather than looking at it. This is how the animals look for you . . . Anything that is out of the natural order, movement, shadow, or noise attracts their attention and they focus on it."

DISCOVER THE LOST ART OF FINDING YOUR WAY

Why do some people have a good sense of direction, while others don't?

Migrating birds and fish use the earth's magnetic fields to navigate home. A British study in 1980 suggested that humans have the same ability, called magnetoreception. That theory remains unproved, but as *Backpacker* magazine reports, a study of "noninstrument navigation" by Polynesians suggested "these highly skilled route-finders may turn to their magnetoreception abilities for orientation when cues like the sun and stars are unavailable." Ben Finney, PhD, professor of anthropology at the University of Hawaii, told the magazine, "We are likely born with this innate sense, and then either develop it as we age or lose it from lack of use." Another recent theory holds that humans have so-called "grid cells" in our brains that keep track of where we are, even when we can't see landmarks.

That GPS unit in the car is useful to families, and can be a real boon to wilderness trekkers, but recent research suggests that the more we use GPS devices, the less ability we have to create mental maps of where we are, or have been, or will be. The point here isn't the overuse of GPS, but the underuse of our inborn neglected super-senses, possibly including magnetoreception. Certainly several of our senses, including proprioception (our body position sense), are enhanced when we spend more time outside.

Here are some ways for kids and adults to rediscover the art of finding our way home—to become natural navigators. Some use the senses, including common sense, and others employ natural knowledge.

Strengthen your inner GPS.

In everyday life, periodically ignore the compass in your car and practice sensing north, south, east, and west. Make that a road-trip game for the family. Before your family heads for the hills, study topological maps to get the lay of the land. When you're hiking, consciously note every landmark and turn in the trail. The brain does better with spatial relationships when it's well rested, so get plenty of sleep before a trip.

Learn to read signposts of land, water, and sky.

Kids and adults can explore a rich literature about reading the signs of nature, one that goes beyond the basics of tracking or reading animal signs. Among the most fascinating sources along this line are the recently published book *The Lost Art of Finding Our Way*, by Harvard physics professor John Edward Huth, and the classic *Finding Your Way Without Map or Compass*, by Harold Gatty. For example, if you're at sea, luminescence in the water can sometimes indicate a reef or a shoreline. Cloud formations can indicate mountain peaks otherwise unseen beyond the horizon, and features of land, water, and ice can be reflected on the undersides of clouds. The Aldo Leopold Foundation offers a collection of tools and resources for reading the stories the land tells.

Let plants and animals show the way.

It's common knowledge that moss grows on the north side of trees. Actually, it's not that simple — it depends on how much shade is available from other trees, the degree of dampness, and which hemisphere you're in (in the southern hemisphere, moss tends to grow on the south side of trees). But the mystery of direction is rich in plant and animal clues. For example, Harold Gatty points to "signpost ants," creatures so particular about how they build their nests and mounds that people lost in a fog can study them to find their bearing.

Study the constellations.

In particular, learn where the North Star is, in relation to other constellations. "If you find yourself lost in the wilderness — or out at sea — a few useful star navigation techniques can help you find the way again," recommends the Appalachian Mountain Club. "Celestial navigation draws on the placement of the stars to infer location and it remains one of the best ways to find your north-south position. The key is to use the angles between the stars and the horizon to locate your position on the globe." Learn more about celestial navigation at Outdoors.org.

Use an old-fashioned but never-out-of-date compass and map.

A compass isn't low-tech, and it's not high-tech. Think of it as *mid-tech*. The floating-needle compass is basic; fancier compasses may come with built-in magnifying glasses for reading maps, or a clinometer, which gauges the angle of a mountain slope.

Take a course in basic navigation or orienteering.

The use of a map and compass for navigation is called orienteering. Choose a course that offers good field practice to build skills and confidence. The REI Outdoor School offers such classes at many REI stores, as do local mountaineering and outdoor organizations. The Boy Scouts and Girl Scouts offer merit badges in orienteering.

🌿 **Take up the sport of orienteering or rogaining.**
Orienteering is the sport of outdoor racing using a map and compass, and it's available to people of all ages. Orienteering USA offers information about the increasingly sophisticated sport, which can be conducted on foot, skis, and mountain bikes. Australia's Sydney Olympic Park calls orienteering "space racing," and organizes races for kids, described as "part treasure hunt, part fun run . . . [Y]ou have forty-five minutes to get to as many checkpoints as you can using a specially produced orienteering map." Rogaining (not to be confused with the race to regain hair growth) involves competitive, long distance, cross-country navigation on foot.

🌿 **For nautical navigation, use a sextant.**
A more complex mid-tech device is the sextant, a handheld instrument used for nautical navigation by measuring angles between a star or planet and the horizon. Electronic navigation is convenient and generally accurate, but "it continues to be vulnerable enough that it would be folly to abandon the practice of taking sights routines," writes Comdr. Bruce A. Bauer, USN (ret.), author of *The Sextant Handbook*. "Off the Atlantic coast recently our radar, loran, and single sideband radio all were smoked in one brilliant instant by a lightning stroke merely near our vessel — not even a hit."

🌿 **Learn even more about reading the natural world.**
We can develop the specific knowledge that comes from reading the natural environment. To learn more about navigating using natural phenomena and innate human abilities, read Harvard physicist John Edward Huth's fascinating book, *The Lost Art of Finding Our Way*. Also, *Keepers of the Animals: Native American Stories and Wildlife Activities for Children* offers a rich array of techniques appropriate for children, teens, and adults. Much of the knowledge of indigenous people about navigation and tracking, however, is

probably not transferrable to the rest of us. As Ailton Kenak of the Krenaki tribe in Brazil has said, "All the knowledge of our people is based on a permanent relationship with the places in which we live." But learning is also a form of action. GaiaFoundation.org is a good source of information on how indigenous peoples know the world.

TRY A LITTLE MINDFULNESS

The best trackers, wildlife photographers, and hunters practice mindfulness, though they may not call it that. A more meaningful experience in the natural world requires paying deep, moment-by-moment attention not only to what's around you, but also to how our bodies, minds, and, yes, souls, are taking it all in—and setting aside judgment. Research suggests that people who get outdoors in nature tend to have high moment-to-moment awareness, less stress, reduced anxiety and depression—and parents who practice mindfulness report greater happiness with their parenting skills. Here are a few ways that parents, children, and other folks can practice mindfulness.

🍃 **Use newly activated natural senses to experience life more deeply.**

Journalist Mark Stevens, on MomScape.com, suggests that parents and teachers help children notice different intensities of experience: "The varying strength of air blowing on leaves will teach your child the joys of the subtle differences of sound intensity floating into their ears . . . The smells of wood or a passing skunk can excite the smallest of explorers and teach them the effects of differing wind direction or dampness. Sticks and stones come in many shapes, sizes and consistency. Once your children appreciate the diversity below their feet, each outing into nature will be a joyous occasion."

❧ Pick a "sit spot."

Jon Young, one of the world's preeminent nature educators, and coauthor of *Coyote's Guide*, advises children and adults to find a special place in nature, whether it's under a tree at the end of the yard, a hidden bend of a creek, or a rooftop garden. "Know it by day; know it by night; know it in the rain and in the snow, in the depth of winter and in the heat of summer," he writes. "Know the birds that live there, know the trees they live in. Get to know these things as if they were your relatives . . . That is the most important thing you can do in order to excel at any skill in nature." While finding a sit spot may seem most appropriate for smaller children, adults and teenagers can benefit, too. Everyone can use a special place away from peer, academic, and relationship pressures.

❧ Encourage kids to do a silent solo sit at school or home.

Here's a paradoxical activity: group solitude. Parents, family nature clubs, or hiking programs can follow IslandWood's lead. Guides at the organization's 225-acre outdoor learning center on Bainbridge Island in Washington State take groups of a dozen or more children and adults on hikes through the forest. Some of these hikers have never been alone in the woods. Prior to the hike, the guides place notes on trees or rocks along the way. Each hiker is encouraged to stay a few hundred yards apart, and to read the notes, which suggest things like, "For three minutes, be still. What do you hear or smell?" Variations of this activity can be used at school or closer to home.

❧ Go on an awareness walk.

The practice of an "awareness walk" is similar to Jon Young's sit spot and IslandWood's silent solo sit, but with more emphasis on walking meditation. Jini Reddy, in an article for the *Telegraph* in the UK, writes about walking through the dunes of a national nature reserve: "Ordinarily on such an outing, I'd be chattering away with friends, loaded down with beach gear. But today I'm light-footed and as silent as a ghost," she writes. "I can see my companions, as we're all walking in single file, a discreet distance from each other. Have we dramatically fallen out? Perish the thought: we've all signed up for a day of mindful walking." Such walks are hosted by such organizations as Wilderness Minds, which encourages people to stop, look, and listen more attentively to nature—and to themselves.

Practice mindfulness with a family or friendship nature club.

In addition to activating and expanding underused senses, being mindful in nature offers families and friends an opportunity for calm and intimacy. Chiara D'Amore received her doctorate in the Sustainability Education program at Prescott College, and is founder of Columbia Families in Nature in Columbia, Maryland. She's also conducting a study of family nature clubs. D'Amore says family nature clubs offer a chance to be mindful. Family members can take "that minute to stop and be mindful about what is around them, what they hear, what they see, how their body feels." Such moments are both powerful and calming. "Instead of shouting at your children, you can take a deep breath and re-presence oneself in life and bring that into your parenting and your family," says D'Amore. "Not just the parents, the children are also getting this."

HIGH-TECH,
HIGH-NATURE?

· ·

I gniting underutilized senses can make everyday experience
richer, and can have practical application in school and at work.
And it can impress friends. "A good pathfinder can become so
proficient that he can amaze the average person. If he likes to be mysterious, he can easily persuade his friends that he has a sixth sense,"
wrote Harold Gatty. But, as he pointed out, the "sixth sense" isn't so
much about magic as it is about the heightened use of our senses and
a deeper knowledge of the natural world—the Extranet.

This is not to say that digital technology isn't useful outdoors.
Developing a Hybrid Mind also includes the use of technology in
nature.

Tech happens. It can be a formidable barrier-to-nature experience.
But to be fair, a list of bad tech side effects, like the warning labels on
the packaging of pharmaceuticals, does not tell the full story. The
point isn't that technology is bad for kids or the rest of us, but that
daily, monthly, yearly, lifelong *electronic immersion, without a force to
balance it*, can drain our ability to pay attention, to think clearly, to
be productive and creative.

The truth is, we've always used technology to get outside. A fishing
rod is technology. So are binoculars, compasses, and a backpack.
Children and adults always have the option of using the traditional,

mid-tech gear, but high-tech/high-nature families also grab newer inventions on their way out the door.

These enhancements needn't get in the way of the experience. For families, the trick is to maintain an emphasis on direct experience, and use digital technology when it's appropriate, in a way that doesn't block the senses of the user or the people nearby.

GO WILDSNAPPING

For children, teenagers, and adults, wildlife and landscape photography is a great way to experience nature. Digital cameras dramatically reduce the cost of taking experimental photos of birds, worms, beetles, and small feet. Smartphones can also be used. "Taking camera-toting children into nature—whether in their own backyards, walking through a woods, or visiting a state or national park—catalyzes visual creativity," says photographer David FitzSimmons, author of the book *Curious Critters*. "One of the most beneficial aspects of taking pictures is how it helps fine-tune our vision."

● Start simply.

True, wildlife photography can become costly, but in the beginning, using a small digital camera focused through one eyepiece of a pair of binoculars can work well. Digital Photography Review offers recommendations for kid-friendly digital cameras. Start with a disposable camera if you're worried about the child handling a regular one. Aldo Leopold, the great conservationist and author of the classic *Sand County Almanac*, was an accomplished photographer. The South Dakota Leopold Education Project offers a free download of the basic guide, *Capturing the Digital Landscape*.

● Make a family or kid click list for a photo scavenger hunt.

Create a list of natural items to take photos of someday; then collect photos of as many of them as possible. Make this a competition among family members, neighborhood kids, or classmates. NatureRocks.org offers tips for a photo scavenger hunt. Capture the seasons, and don't forget to look up. Take photos of the sky from the same spot each day and make a photo collage.

GoPro where you go.

Young people are particularly good at this adventure, which involves attaching a small movie camera to the body, and recording your outdoor adventure. YouTube is crowded with sometimes harrowing videos by outdoor athletes, usually young, of mountain biking, fishing, and all manner of extreme outdoor sports. GoPro cameras can also be used for quieter nature pastimes, like crawling behind a turtle to record its view of the world.

Post your "digital catch" online or publish it in a DIY book.

On your own website, Facebook page, or in an old-fashioned scrapbook, collect your family nature photos in one place. Or create a printed book by using one of the online services that help you design and publish, in limited edition, your own hardback or paperback photo book.

Download a digital nature guide.

The best apps can enhance your experiences in nature. Common Sense Media, a trusted site that rates media for children, lists some wonderful apps for exploring the outdoors. For example, Leafsnap .com, an electronic field guide, encourages young people to take photos of trees and identify them using visual recognition software. Leafsnap also has games to enhance tree-identification skills. There are numerous apps that, using geotracking, help kids explore the night sky in real time, as well as provide a wealth of information about the cosmos. You might also want to install a compass app, to encourage orienteering skills, a neglected skill in the GPS era.

BE A SOUNDCATCHER

Anyone in the family can become a nature soundcatcher, a recordist who gathers sound samples from the wild. The bar to entry into what used to be a much-less-affordable hobby has been lowered. If you want to capture sounds of birds, animals, or other nature phenomena, you can now do so with relatively inexpensive digital gear. Two good sources about nature recording are All About Birds and the Wildlife Recording Society.

🍃 **Listen to the heartbeat of a tree.**
Place a contact microphone, one that picks up vibrations directly from physical objects instead of air ($15 and up at a music store) in the hollow of a tree and notice the different sounds. Help your children check their tree's "heartbeat" from time to time; make these "checkups" part of their role as tree adopter. A recommended book is *The Bumper Book of Nature*.

🍃 **Attend a Concert of the "Great Animal Orchestra."**
Bernie Krause, author of *The Great Animal Orchestra: Finding the Origins of Music in the World's Wild Places*, is an internationally known recorder of nature sounds (and a former sound engineer for the Rolling Stones). He recommends that young people (and the rest of us) become acquainted with biophony, the sounds of living organisms. "Get up just as it is getting light and open up your window," he advises. "See if you can identify what birds, insects, or amphibians you hear by sound alone." With a small digital recorder, record them.

🍃 **Use cell phones to record nature sounds.**
Sound recorders are the hearing equivalent of using binoculars to sharpen and bring into close focus the visual world, according to Krause. He encourages fourth and fifth graders in urban areas to use their own or their parents' cell phones to go on nature-recording expeditions independently or in small teams. He asks

them to bring back the sound of, say, a robin. The kids often bring back recordings filled with the sounds of cars, planes, helicopters, powered garden tools — all of which tend to mask the sound of the robin (and other critters' voices). "I gently point out the noise factor in their recording and ask them to repeat the exercise . . . this time without human noise," he says. Over time, the kids figure out that the best times to record are in the spring and early summer around dawn . . . the "magic hour," as Krause calls it. The kids learn how to identify the song of a robin; that there is a lot of noise in their environment; and how to use a specific tool to capture natural sound. "And they learn that the natural world has a voice or a narrative that needs to express itself."

Graduate to more-sophisticated recording gear.

Beyond the cell phone, the least expensive entry-level nature-recording options are digital voice recorders that can connect to computers. When a child or young person is ready to step up to better quality, there are also a number of more professional options in the $100–$300 range. The two basic types of microphones used for nature-sound recording are parabolic and shotgun microphones. Parabolic mics are more precise and are also easier for a beginner to learn to use. Headphones need to be good enough to monitor the sound without too much quality loss. Another option: buy a plug-in smartphone microphone.

Do a noise study of the neighborhood.

Once families, kids, or adults are proficient with recording gear, they can create a sound map of the neighborhood, and compare it to a park, wilderness, or a cityscape. "This is one very good way to find out how we are affecting the natural world around us and, in particular, how well the creatures who live near us are able to communicate," says Krause. "And you can do this without doing any damage or further affecting the behavior of urban wildlife." Krause is concerned that, because of human noise, we're running out of places where you can hear the sounds of other life, or silence, without the interference of human noise. You can listen to his recordings of the dawn biophony and learn more about his work on his Facebook page.

🌿 To app or not to app.

Birding apps for smartphones attract young eyes, and they're useful for species identification or study at home, as long as those eyes don't get stuck in the app. Also note that the American Birding Association suggests that birders limit the use of bird apps that play bird sounds for identification, especially in areas with high bird populations, or for attracting species that are threatened, endangered or rare. "Here's the rule followed by many," according to *National Geographic*. "If in doubt, err on the side of the bird, and keep your phone in your pocket."

🌿 Turn the sound off. Stop, look, and listen.

Be a good digital citizen, say Michele Whiteaker, copublisher of NaturePlayTrips.com, and Diana Graber, cofounder of Cyberwise.org, an online hub that helps adults understand the digital world. "Part of the nature experience is silence and wild sounds," they write. "No one wants to hear the *click, click, click* of texting or taking photos. If you'd rather hear music on the trail, wear headphones. Nature is a sacred place to those who are enjoying it *and* the wildlife that calls it home. Do your best not to interrupt their experience."

🌿 Cache and release.

Geocaching is an increasingly popular way to encourage kids to explore the outdoors. Adults or older kids place prizes—for example, polished rocks, puzzle games, compasses—in containers, then put them in hiding places in a park or other outdoor environment. The items should be hidden but still slightly visible. Go to Geocaching.com to register the coordinates of the cache, or to find a preexisting cache. Using a handheld GPS unit or a smartphone with a GPS or geocaching app, children or their adult companions navigate their way to the coordinates and look around. This is a great way to get kids interested in the outdoors. An electronic treasure hunt can be an easier sell than some outdoor activities.

🍃 Can't go outside today?
Be an electronic wildlife watcher.

Thanks to the U.S. Fish & Wildlife Service and the National Conservation Training Center, you can watch, in real time, a bald eagle nest. The web offers many opportunities to view live nature cams. It's one of many online sites for virtual wildlife viewing. CelebrateUrbanBirds.org provides links to birdcams.

🍃 Use a bookending strategy.

Michele Whiteaker and Diana Graber recommend a "bookending" strategy. When a family arrives at a hiking trail or other outdoor destination, she encourages everyone to use their tech gear for a while, but then asks them to put the electronics away during the rest of the outing. She encourages families to share their photos and other digital discoveries when they get home. The bookending approach allows people to enjoy a pure nature experience and have their tech, too.

🍃 Give kids a choice; you might be surprised.

During a summer science program at Mohonk Preserve in New Paltz, New York, kids were given a choice between using traditional (pads of paper, pencils, old-fashioned compasses, and so forth) and high-tech tools to explore and record nature experiences. Overwhelmingly, the kids preferred the low-tech and mid-tech tools.

🍃 Even tech tycoons agree: unplug often.

It's surprising how many technology leaders own off-the-grid cabin retreats. They know they need time to reboot, and that time in nature stimulates their creativity. For their own kids, some technology leaders have adopted these limits: thirty minutes to two hours of tablet or smartphone use a day; allow ten- to fourteen-year-olds to use computers on school nights, but only for homework; make a distinction between consuming and creating on these devices. A *New York Times* reporter once asked Apple's Steve Jobs, "So, your kids must love the iPad?" His answer: "They haven't used it. We limit how much technology our kids use at home."

The Techno-Fast

O n the way out of town one day, I got the shakes. Well, not the shakes exactly, but I wasn't a happy pre-camper.

My wife and I had committed to four days away from beeping gadgets, ringing phones, leaf-blowing neighbors, the on-demand life. It had been too long since our last immersion in the natural world. We were going on a techno-fast.

My computer was set to send out this e-mail auto-reply: "I'm taking a brief break from all communications electronic . . . OK, here goes. Pulling the plug . . ."

For emergencies, we brought Kathy's minimalistic not-so-smart cell phone but planned to leave it in the car, turned off.

My laptop, iPhone, and iPad stayed home.

"What's wrong?" Kathy asked, glancing at me.

Maybe I looked like I had eels in my shirt. Tech withdrawal.

We were on our way to a rental cabin on Palomar Mountain, east of San Diego. The cabin was beyond cell phone or Internet reception, or so we hoped.

The winding road led us away from the stucco wastelands into golden hills and blue-gray live oaks. We watched a red-tailed hawk balance on a swaying electric line, and farther to the east, the cumulus clouds on their afternoon ascent. As often happens when we head for the mountains, in recent years and when our boys were younger, we felt a weight lift.

No matter what our age, we pay a price for too much tech, and it's not wholesale.

"A growing body of research shows that juggling many tasks, as so many people do in this technological era, can divide attention and hurt learning and performance," *New York Times* blogger Matt Richtel writes, reporting on a study published in the Proceedings of the National Academy of Sciences. Experiencing too many "senior moments" lately? "We now understand that this is not necessarily a memory problem per se, but often the result of an interaction between attention and memory," according to Adam Gazzaley, a neurologist at the University of California at San Francisco.

Getting more music, art, yoga, meditation, weight-lifting—whatever—into our lives can help. But technology fasting while spending time in the natural world may be the most effective antidote.

In the 1970s, environmental psychologists Rachel and Stephen Kaplan began foundational work in the study of nature's healing effect on the mind. Their studies suggested that contact with nature can assist with recovery from mental fatigue and can help restore attention. Meaningful contact with nature can also help reboot the brain's ability to think. And it excites the senses.

But unplugging the power strip doesn't always come naturally, even for those of us who, by nature, love nature. It requires a conscious act and a change of scenery.

These days, finding sanctuary is becoming harder. Many parks and campgrounds now offer Wi-Fi—the theory being that people just won't get outdoors if they can't stay connected. For sanity, we need No Wi-Fi Zones and Phone-Silent Sanctuaries, especially for families who can't afford a cabin on private land.

As it turned out, wireless signals did reach the wilds of Palomar. Now and then, Kathy and I looked up from our books, interrupted by the sound of a cell phone ringing somewhere in the forest.

Even so, by the fourth day, we were surprisingly calm. Taking a break helped; doing it in a more natural habitat helped even more.

On our last day, we drove to a pond. I fly-fished for an hour as Kathy sat under the trees and read the last chapter of another book. Then we wound our way back down the mountain, already thinking about our next techno-fast.

NATURAL CREATIVITY: DO IT, BUILD IT, PAINT IT, PLAY IT

· ·

O ur senses are the scouts of our creativity. Nature stimulates the senses and invites creativity through the complexity of possibilities for play and learning and work, through a kind of osmosis, through ecstatic experiences. Children soak up their environments, so it makes sense to ensure that the environment of play is as rich as possible. The body of research on nature's impact on creativity is growing. A Danish study found that outdoor kindergartens were better than indoor schools at stimulating children's creativity. The University of Kansas concluded that young people show significant cognitive improvement and a 50 percent boost in creativity after living for a few days steeped in nature.

"We think that it peaks after about three days of really getting away, turning off the cell phone, not hauling the iPad and not looking for Internet coverage," according to researcher Ruth Ann Atchley, associate professor of cognitive/clinical psychology at the University of Kansas. "It's when you have an extended period of time surrounded by that softly fascinating environment that you start seeing all kinds of positive effects in how your mind works."

Play experts and psychologists have long believed that the most creative environments are the ones with the most loose parts. Nature is filled with an infinite number of loose parts, which children dismantle and reassemble into new realities.

Small Projects for Small Hands

🍂 **Create your own spider web or flower.**
Here's how kids can make a spider web out of sticks and string. Or invent their own flower. Collect a few flowers of different species (preferably not from a neighbor's flower bed) and disassemble them at home. Combine the stems, petals, seeds, and leaves in any pattern that appeals. Glue the creation to a piece of paper when finished. Kids also can use pictures from magazines.

🍂 **Make your own potpourri.**
Gather and air-dry fragrant petals and mix them in a nonmetallic bowl, adding a teaspoon of orris root (available online) per cup of flowers, if desired, to make potpourri last longer. Place the mix into drawstring bags, or circles of netting tied with ribbons, or use in bowls to scent rooms and drawers.

🍂 **Make your own perfume.**
Your kids can collect fragrant flowers and herbs and combine them on a piece of waxed paper. Fold the paper over and crush the ingredients with a mallet or rolling pin. Put the ingredients in a container with a cup of water, seal, and let it sit for a few hours. Pour the mixture through a strainer and simmer in a saucepan on the stove for a few minutes. (Never leave small children unsupervised in the kitchen.) Bottle the creation and enjoy its natural scent. Education .com offers complete instructions.

🌿 **Create a sand castle or village, and sand people, and then crown yourself. Naturally.**

All that's needed is some sand—in a sandbox or at a beach or shore—and a water source. Children can form wet sand into shapes using hands, cans, containers, buckets, or commercial molds, getting as detailed as desired. Youngsters can dig a moat around their castle and let it fill with water naturally, or fill it themselves. British children at beaches build sandmen in the form of snowmen. One can use sticks, seaweed, pebbles, and shells as adornments. Then, kids can coronate themselves king or queen of the beach or forest. Play England recommends using a length of paper or cardboard as the base of a crown, to be adorned with leaves, feathers, shells, and other nature jewels. Not included: loyal subjects.

🌿 **Make a mini-pond.**

Using little more than a tub, sand, a few rocks, and some water, WildlifeWatch.org.uk shows how to make a small oasis for aquatic and amphibious backyard creatures. Dig a hole large enough to accommodate the tub, put down a layer of sand at the bottom of the hole, place the tub inside, and fill any gaps with sand or dirt. Then, stack rocks up one side of the tub, from the bottom to the rim, so that anything that falls in can get out. Fill the tub with water and wait to see life take hold. Add a goldfish or other small fish to keep mosquitoes from breeding in the water. Frogs and turtles are also welcome. A few duckweeds, which look something like miniature lily pads, will entice other creatures to come near.

More Challenging Construction Projects

🌿 **Whittle this.**

Whittling is a traditional nature-based pastime. Take most of the risk out of the equation for children by having them use a vegetable peeler instead of a knife. Perhaps design and make a walking stick: Find a stick that is at least higher than your child's waist, snap off any twigs on the shaft, and whittle the top into a bear's head or other nature shape. Your kids can carve designs on the shaft; decorate with yarn, beads, and found nature objects.

🌿 Bend your own bow, chip your own arrowheads.

Make arrowheads by chipping away at a flat piece of flint until it's sharp (be sure eye protection is in place), affix to a straight stick stripped of bark or a craft dowel, and glue strips of feather to the opposite end at 120-degree angles, leaving enough space for your fingers. Select a strong but flexible sapling for the bow, less than three-quarters of an inch thick. Taper the ends and cut two small notches on each tip. Attach a nylon string with the appropriate knots. When shooting the arrows, be sure you and your children wear a glove on your bow hands.

🌿 Launch a frog raft.

Take a small plank of wood and drive a nail through it at one end. Your children can help or older kids may work alone, or assist younger children. Slide a candle onto the nail. Mount a screw with an eye ring into the board at the other end, then attach a long length of string or fishing line to the eye ring. The ingenious folks at HowStuffWorks.com suggest the next steps: Go to a pond at night and use a flashlight to spot frogs (their eyes refract light); then light the candle and push the board out into the water toward the frogs, holding on to the string to retrieve the board. Wait and watch; the frogs may jump onto the board to investigate the light. For more information, go to HowStuffWorks.com.

🌿 Create a rope swing.

There are many variations on the rope swing, but the easiest to set up is a simple rope tied to a tree branch strong enough to support an adult's full body weight. Use a strong rope, an equivalent length of twine with a weight on one end, a couple of appropriate knots, something for a seat, and you and your kids are in business. For illustrated instructions, go to Instructables.com.

🌿 **Build an owl box, or assemble an owl box kit.**
Owl boxes provide cavity-nesting species like screech owls a place
to safely raise their young. Be willing to clean the box at least once a
year. *Audubon* magazine offers instructions on how to build an owl
box, which is one way to encourage these useful rodent-catchers
to stay in the area.

🌿 **Make a telescope or magnifying glass.**
To get a closer look at nature, your kids can make a magnifying
glass with water. Cut a circle out of a two-liter bottle, from the
curved part of the neck. Fill the plastic disc with water and, voilà,
magnifying glass. Children can make a telescope out of toilet paper
tubes and magnifying lenses, popped out of a magnifying glass. Cut
one tube lengthwise and tape it back together so it fits into a second
tube. Tape a lens to both open ends and slide the tubes to focus.
Make an underwater scope by using a rubber band to attach plastic wrap over one end of an aluminum can that has both ends open.
Submerge the wrapped end. Suggested book: *This Book Was a Tree*.
Find detailed instructions for making a telescope at Instructables
.com. For making a magnifying glass, see JustMommies.com.

🌿 **Build a fort, hut, den, or playhouse.**
Parents or other adults can provide the raw materials, including
sticks, boards, blankets, boxes, ropes, and nails, but it's best when
kids are the architects and builders. Impromptu dens or playhouses can be made using tarps, old blankets, rugs, and sticks. Or
make a mini-den out of branches, leaves, and other natural materials. Mini-dens can also be visited by pets, dolls, and imaginary
friends. *Shelters, Shacks & Shanties: The Classic Guide to Building
Wilderness Shelters*, by Daniel C. Beard, is a turn-of-the-last-
century guide to building lean-tos, dugout forts, and other perfect
places. For more insight and inspiration, read *Children's Special
Places*, by David Sobel.

🍃 **Help your kids build a tree house.**

Tree houses can be as simple as a platform a few feet above ground or as sophisticated as multistory tree condos with their own ziplines and rope bridges. Be selective about the tree your kids choose. It should be a mature (not elderly) hardwood strong enough to support the weight, with deep roots and no disease. Build so the weight of the structure is as centered over the trunk as possible, and leave gaps to accommodate tree growth. Research proper safety and construction techniques before you start. And check your local regulations and homeowner agreement. Ideally, as with forts, huts, and dens, parents can provide the lumber and equipment, then step back and let the kids design and build the tree house. (It's to be their creation; don't worry about aesthetics.)

🍃 **Tree houses aren't just for kids anymore.**

In recent years, more adults have started building complex, sophisticated tree houses for themselves, or as backyard getaways for the whole family. Some are works of art. Suggested books: *Tree Houses You Can Actually Build* and *Be in a Treehouse.* A number of books are available for adult-oriented tree houses, including *New Treehouses of the World* and *Treehouses and Playhouses You Can Build.*

What Kids Learn
by Building
Tree Houses and Forts—
If Adults Let Them

••••••••••••••••••••••••••••••••••

I n 2014, Kansas City's KCTV News reported on a group of neighborhood kids in Lee's Summit who "learned a hard lesson about city codes." These kids had built a fine fort on a vacant lot (a stone's throw from where my boyhood friends and I built a three-story tree house), using scrap lumber left over from the construction of surrounding homes, the same way generations of children had done before. Responding to an anonymous complaint about the fort, building inspectors sent a bulldozer to demolish the fort, despite a written plea made by the youngsters:

> *Dear City, Please do not tear this house down! We have all worked for almost a year on it, for hours and hours. We have all had fun climbing on it, camping in it, having picnics in it. Many happy memories were forged here. We all hope that it won't be torn down. So please don't tear it down!*

The fault herein does not lie with city officials—they're just doing their jobs—but with the codes and restrictions, common throughout the nation. These constraints spring from two public and private mandates: be neat; be safe. Never mind another kind of danger: the stunting of creativity and inventiveness and the kind of risk taking necessary for healthy development and true learning.

Sadly, this is part of the creeping criminalization of natural play.

Yet, the young can learn so much from fort and tree house building, especially if most of the construction is by their own hand. They can learn about the most common sizes of plywood and studs, about the sizes of nails and the difference between nails and screws. They can learn that diagonal bracing stiffens structure, that framing must strengthen windows or trapdoors, that the slope of the roof will shed or hold rain. They can learn about measurement and three-dimensional geometry. They can learn about the size of their body related to the world, and about the height from which they can safely jump, and about failure and success, and, as my architect friend Alberto Lau points out, that they can solve a complex problem by breaking it down into smaller, simpler problems—a skill useful in engineering, art, and life.

Discover the Art of Nature

🍃 **Wear nature on your sleeve.**
Your kids can capture the unique patterns on the undersides of leaves by gathering leaves with unusual shapes and textures, painting them thoroughly, and then pressing them onto a T-shirt, piece of paper, or other object, and gently lifting to create a print. Or kids can make a flower chain bracelet. Suggest collecting dandelions, clovers, or other common flowers to make a chain, says Sara St. Antoine, author of young adult fiction. "Make a small slit in the stem of one flower and slide the stem of another flower through up to its head. Continue linking one flower to the next until you have a long enough loop for a bracelet, necklace, or tiara." Or make bracelets out of inside-out duct tape; kids can attach leaves, twigs, feathers and other cool stuff they find along the trail.

🍃 **Create art with found nature.**
Art supplies can be expensive. You can let nature supply them for free. Some ideas: a temporary sculpture with rocks, sticks, leaves, and other items; a stack of precariously balanced round stones can turn into mysterious cairns, or markers. By gathering objects in nature and sticking them onto a soft ball of clay, as the book *I Love My World* suggests, anyone can create his or her own natural art piece or invent an imaginary creature. Call it a "blobster."

🍃 **Make your own paint.**

Children can make their own paints from walnuts, berries, and clay. Gather leaves, dirt, and berries (be sure they're nonpoisonous), add water, mash into a paint, and let the masterpieces flow. According to the instructions on Education.com, dye can be created from walnut shells by soaking them overnight, boiling them for two hours, and straining out the shells.

🍃 **Paint with mud.**

Help children mix dirt and water in a bucket; then offer them a paintbrush to paint with mud on pavement. Directions: Go outside, and sketch a scene with pencil on a canvas of cardboard or paper plate. Smear on different colors of clay to create mountains, sunsets, rivers. They can use various implements, such as forks, to give the clay texture. Or fashion clay into a "bog it," a fantastical creature that originated in England. Add mud goblins and fairies. Leave them to stand guard over nature. Suggested books: *Nature Seeker Workbook, I Love My World, The Nature Connection.*

🍃 **Create art with the sun.**

Show kids how to use shadows to trace people and objects on the sidewalk. Or make silhouette prints on paper. Place a flower or other natural object on paper, preferably commercial "sun-print paper," available in craft or art stores, cover it with clear plastic (usually included with the sun-print paper), and leave it out in the sun. Results change when the sun is at different angles throughout the day.

🍃 **Make flower press art.**

Press flowers and leaves into a thick book, or even better, use a flower press. To make one, place flowers on newspaper or blotter paper (available at craft stores). Insert corrugated cardboard between layers of plant and paper. Enclose the layers in squares of particle board or wood and secure this "sandwich" with a belt, bungee cord, or C-clamp. Art projects can follow results of flower pressings. KidsGardening.org offers more detailed instructions for pressing flowers.

Make natural musical instruments.

Sticks and stones can break bones, but your kids can also play them. Sticks, rocks, and other natural objects are great for percussion instruments. For a rattle, pebbles or dry seed pods in a cup work well. A blade of grass held taut between the bases and tips of your thumbs makes sounds when you blow. Kids can have fun conducting an outdoor concert, with a chorus of birds and crickets.

Create a Family Nature-Trail Guide

∙∙∙∙∙∙∙∙∙∙∙∙∙∙∙∙∙∙∙∙∙∙∙∙∙∙∙∙∙∙∙∙∙∙∙∙∙

Educator Tamra Willis and her husband, Mike Pelton, a wildlife biologist and bear researcher, helped their young grandchildren develop nearby nature trail guides. The children then appointed themselves "trail guides" for other kids.

"Choose a trail close to home (park, wooded area, bike path), and together study aspects of the trail that the children can share with others," Willis says.

Research the history, biology, and geology of the area. Study maps of the trail to learn about distance, topography, elevation. Hike the trail and discover what animals live along it. Look for and document animal signs or homes, and teach the kids to identify birds along the trail by sight and song. Take local field guides, and rely, too, on your family's own observations. Find out what happened along or near that trail in history: who built the structures or fences, or paved the trail. Record predominant rock types and rock formations; what trees and plants are located close to the trail; which plants have medicinal qualities; which are native or nonnative species.

Then have the kids create a brochure or website about the trail. Include stories related to your family's or each child's personal experiences along the trail. Share the knowledge with others, and encourage your kids or grandchildren to become volunteer trail guides. This project can be used by parents or teachers, and can easily be adapted for any school-age child. "Not only does this activity provide practice in research and reading," says Willis, "but the presentations as a trail expert can be a major confidence booster for young children."

Nature Writing

🍃 **Keep a nature journal.**

Encourage kids to keep a record of their nature experiences by writing or drawing, or combining both, on paper or as a blog. You can, too. Good guides on nature-journaling are available to help children, teenagers, and families record their outdoor discoveries in words, drawings, and photographs. Recommended books: *My Nature Journal* and *Keeping a Nature Journal*.

🍃 **Write about the beauty of something ugly.**

Environmental educator Clifford Knapp likes to issue this challenge: Have kids select something in the environment that at first seems ugly or unsightly. Then they can write a story about that object, describing how it is beautiful. For example, a dragonfly can seem strange up close, but notice how the translucent wings look like leaded windows, and how the body on some can be as bright as a jewel.

🍃 **Create rock art or pebble poetry.**

Paint rocks with original designs. Kids can collect smooth, flat stones and use markers to write one word on each; then they can arrange and rearrange them to create a poem. If they want to preserve the stones, apply a coat of varnish. Or, keep it simple: they can write poems or paint pictures on a large pebble or rock.

🍃 **Spend a half hour outdoors; write an instant nature essay.**

Parents, teachers, and other adults can do this as well, but it may be especially effective with young people. A California high school biology teacher asked his students to spend a half hour outside—anywhere that they considered part the natural world, whether it was an urban park, a yard, or a stream outside of town—and then write about their experiences. One student left town and got away from exterior lights. "I saw more stars than I have probably ever seen in my entire life," she recalled. Another wrote: "I have never taken so much notice of the smaller things."

🌿 **Go on a haiku hike.**

Haiku, a form of Japanese poetry usually used to write about nature, is simple to compose. Each haiku poem is three lines long. In English, the poem is commonly written with the first line containing five total syllables, the second line containing seven, and the third, five. Take your family members on a hike and write haikus about what they see and then share them.

🌿 **Create handmade books, or self-publish nature fiction or nonfiction books.**

Produce handmade books, possibly using found treasures from the natural world for illustrations, or use your own family's drawing or photos. There are a number of storefront or online services that handle print-on-demand self-publishing. Teenagers, young kids, or adults can do this project together.

These Games (from Around the World) Will Not Be Digitized

🌿 **Rede, Tanzania**

To play rede, players sit in a circle around a mound of sand. An upright stick is plunged into the top of the mound. They then take turns removing a handful of sand from around the stick. When the digging causes the stick to fall over, that player must run to touch a home base — this could be a rock or bare patch — before the others can tag her or him. Set the stick up and start digging again. Once a player is tagged a predetermined number of times, he or she is eliminated from the game.

🌿 **Koabangan, Australia**

This game is ideally played by very young children in an outdoor area with lots of low-growing, bushy trees. To play koabangan, one player hides an object (it can be anything) somewhere in the area while the other players sit with their eyes covered. When the hider gives a signal, the players race to find the object. The person who finds it becomes the new hider.

🌿 Al Saqlah, United Arab Emirates

Dig a hole (it doesn't have to be deep) and partially fill it with pebbles, shells, or marbles. Players of al saqlah take turns throwing a stone in the air and collecting as many of the objects from the hole as they can before catching the stone. They continue doing this until they fail to catch the stone, in which case they return all the objects they had collected on that particular throw. Players take turns until the hole is empty, and the player with the most pebbles/shells/marbles wins.

🌿 Kurukuru, Papua New Guinea

This target-practice game uses the stems of tall, stiff grasses (the game is named for a type of grass), bamboo, sticks, or, for the safety-conscious, pool noodles (noodle-shaped pieces of polyethylene foam, also known as woggles in the UK). Players take turns throwing the sticks like spears, trying to hit an object at a set distance. A hit scores one point. When all players have thrown, they throw again from a greater distance. This continues until nobody can hit the target. The player with the most points wins.

🌿 Marbles Sliding Game, Cree (Native American)

In this traditional Cree game, a dirt slope or snowbank is converted into a ramp for marbles. The ramp should be about five feet long. Players dig twelve small holes at the bottom of the ramp and give them each a different point value. Players take turns trying to accumulate points by rolling a marble down the slope and trying to get it into one of the holes. The winner is the person with the most points. This game is recommended by the website for Family-Games-Treasurehouse.com, as is the next one.

🌿 Ten Sticks, Finland

In this ancient game, a hide-and-seek variation, a board is placed on a stone, and ten small sticks are placed on one side of the board. Someone stomps the board, sending the sticks flying, and a "seeker" has to collect them and put them back on the board before setting out to find the rest of the players.

🌿 Smuggling the geg, Scotland

This game from Scotland is best played in an outdoor area with lots of trees and rocks and other things to hide behind. Draw a four-by-six-foot square in the dirt. This is the "cave." Divide into two teams, the "Outs" (or "Smugglers") and "Ins." The teams must start the game at least thirty feet from each other and from the cave. One of the smugglers secretly holds a "geg," or small object. The In team yells out, "Smugglers!" and then chases the Outs. If an In catches an Out and they don't have the geg, the Out goes free. If the player with the geg makes it to the cave without being caught, the Outs win. If they are caught before they make it, the Ins win.

🌿 More outdoor chase-and-capture games

A chase-and-capture game popular in the streets of Brooklyn in the early twentieth century, ringolievo was a variation of the European game relievo. This game of tag played by two teams involved chalk rings drawn on the street, which served as bases for "prisoners." The game often extended through many city streets. Here's a variation: camouflage tag, in which hiders deck themselves in natural camouflage to hide within sight of the seeker. Or introduce kids to one of the many other variations of tag, such as fainting goat tag or ninja time. Tag is also known as tig and Dobby and Chasey in other parts of the world. Duck duck goose is known as "kho kho" in South Asia, "antoakyire" in Ghana, and "plumpsack" in Germany. Likewise red light, green light is called "cukr, káva, limonáda, čaj, rum, bum!" ("sugar, coffee, lemonade, tea, rum, boom!") in the Czech Republic.

🌿 Playing classic games with natural objects

Most of us have played the classic rock-paper-scissors game. Why not introduce kids to flower rock-paper-scissors, using large flowers to keep score, as they do in Fiji? Every time children lose a round, they pluck a petal from the flower. When they run out of petals, they lose. Or tic-tac-toe. No paper and pencil? No problem. Play this classic boredom buster (which dates back to ancient

Egypt) using natural objects, or kids can make "Xs" out of sticks, using twist ties to hold their shape. Draw the grid on the ground with a stick. See Education.com's example.

The game of graces, Colonial America (by way of France)

More than a century ago, a game called graces was popular. Each child attempted to use a stick to successfully pass a hoop back and forth. This game was devised to promote grace and dexterity in young children. Although hoop-and-stick games are no longer played by contemporary children, the Hula-Hoop, popularized in the 1950s, has maintained its appeal. The Hula-Hoop can be incorporated into many games, including those involving obstacle courses, skipping, and running. Hoop games are good for improving coordination and dexterity.

Webbing

The game of webbing, suggested by Joseph Cornell in *Sharing Nature with Children*, teaches about the interconnectedness of all things in nature. For webbing, kids or adults form a circle. Hand one end of a ball of string to a player and ask her or him to name a plant that grows in the area. Unravel the string and ask if anyone can name an animal that eats that plant. That person then holds on to the string, connecting him or her to the first. Continue asking for interrelated items, such as other animals, shade trees, sun, soil, and water, and unraveling and holding the string to create an ecosystem. Introduce a new element, like a tree falling. Have the tree tug the string, and see how many ultimately feel the tug from that tree.

Predator and prey

Predator and prey must be played carefully with supervision by an adult. It introduces the idea of food chains. Children stand in a circle, about fifteen feet wide. Invite two of the children to stand in the middle and blindfold them. One of them names a local predatory animal, and the other names a species of prey. Both children pretend to be their chosen animal, and the predator must try to "catch" (touch) its quarry using hearing alone. If either wanders too close to the circle's edge, the player should be gently tapped. Also try increasing the number of prey animals, adorning them with bells, or making the circle smaller.

🌿 **Inventing your own nature game**

Researchers have shown that children who play in natural spaces, compared with flat playgrounds or playing fields, are more likely to invent their own games and their own rules—an essential element in developing the capacity for "executive function" in the early years. In West Virginia, Janet Keating and her daughter (when she was small), invented their own game, "the Sound of a Creature Not Stirring"; they would wander through the woods listening for "the sounds they could not hear," and then make a list. For example, sap rising, sunrise, a seed germinating, mitosis, feathers, wood petrifying, a spider weaving its web, a leaf changing color.

Purposeful Play in the Natural World

• •

The psychologist Abraham Maslow, best known for creating Maslow's hierarchy of needs, once said, "Almost all creativity involves purposeful play." Page Lambert, who lives with her family in the mountains west of Denver, Colorado, would agree. For her daughter and son, play was often anchored in work.

"Going to get the sheep in off the meadow should have been a fifteen-minute chore, but my kids' imaginations would lead them (and the dog) to where the wild gooseberries grew in the aspen draw, to the old rusty haying machinery, to the rock pile, and perhaps finally, to the sheep," she recalls. "When they eventually made it back to the barn, I had no doubt that their imaginations had been fully engaged." Lambert, author of *All Things Literary, All Things Natural,* conducts workshops for writers. She believes it's easy to forget how closely connected play and work can or should be. "Children want to have a sense of purpose—it is an innately human need. Give a child a purpose, with meaning, *a reason for which something needs to be done or created.* Define an end goal, and then let the child's imagination figure out how to get there."

She and her neighbors also encouraged their children to pursue another kind of purposeful work/play. "Like painting the wooden street signs for our narrow, dirt roads, or painting the teeter-totter at the playground, or pulling weeds during the community 'weed pulling' day, or yes, helping rake manure from the corral at our community barn before they curry their horse, Maybelline."

Still, Lambert's kids always had time for free-range play.

She recalls how her daughter would explore "the deer paths that meandered in and out of the bur oak woods that surrounded our small log home." From her kitchen window, she could catch glimpses of her daughter, when she was as young as five, "running up the trail, with our dog eagerly running behind her. She would disappear, and reappear, disappear, and reappear. She would arrive back home with leaves in her hair, houndstongue seeds (which, I believe, were the inspiration behind Velcro) stuck to her socks, and usually with a few rocks in her pocket, maybe even a piece of chipped rock. 'Mom, this was from making an arrowhead, right?'" Such play is less related to work, but it does have purpose.

Other Voices

"For older kids, in American Literature, we focus on Thoreau and Emerson. I have them reflect on Transcendentalism by going out into nature alone and without technology, and journaling their thoughts. Many come back to class the next day excited that they were able to 'hear' themselves think without a cell phone."

—Stefanie Crecelius, Sandusky, Ohio

"I no longer see the singularity of my skin tone among my peers as a problem, but instead as a megaphone to give weight to the message that as people of color, people from different ethnic backgrounds, the outdoor world is ours to explore as well. And for those who have grown up connected to and educated in the outdoors, they now have the chance to connect to new cultures, to see flora and fauna through the eyes of city kids."

— CJ Goulding, who has worked with
Washington's North Cascades Institute
to introduce teens from urban
neighborhoods to nature.

"The attitude of 'look but don't touch' and 'nature is too fragile and dangerous' does have its time and place. I get it. I do. We do need to have protected areas. But kids need to have their time and place in nature too. Why can't there be designated areas for nature play, even within protected regions when and where it makes sense?"

—Janice Swaisgood, San Diego, California

"Last night, right before bedtime, my four-year-old daughter wanted to invite us to a 'perfect party' that she was adamantly planning for right that very moment. Not tomorrow, but 'tonight.' This 'perfect party' involved going outside on the porch and gazing at the stars while drawing pictures.

"We could have easily ignored her desires and sent her straight to bed, but we knew there was so much more value in saying yes to her invitation. To be outside gazing at the stars required no more effort than bundling up with jackets and blankets; watching the sky grow dark; and talking about the different moon phases. We seized her interest and made sure to show that we supported her passion right then because I never want to extinguish her flame for the outdoors while it's continuing to grow more bright.

"The key for us is to keep watching for these moments of confidence and support her self-driven outdoor experiences with yes, you can."

*—**Rosanna Nydia Snyder, Seattle, Washington***

Part 3

· ·

The Nature-Rich Home and Garden

"Nature is not a place to visit. It is home."

— GARY SNYDER

*"I want to protect my kids against a dangerous
ignorance of what sustains them. When they help me dig and
hoe the garden . . . they are learning important skills for living
and maintaining life. I have also observed that they appreciate feeling useful. In fact, nearly all the kids I've worked with
on gardening projects get passionate about putting seeds in
the ground, to the point of earnest territoriality."*

— BARBARA KINGSOLVER

EVERYDAY EDEN

. . . .

Your family can create a restorative environment at home. The first step is to do an inventory of the often-overlooked natural elements that already exist in your home and just outside the door. Persistent nature is everywhere—in your yard, on a roof or balcony, sometimes in the most unexpected places.

Look around. Explore the places you *think* you know.

Defining "nature" isn't easy. To some people, nature is *everything*. To others, it's the Grand Canyon or the wren outside the window. Science has tended to leave the definition of nature up to the poets. This lack of a clear designation is one of the prime reasons why scientific research on the impact of nature on human development has been so thin until recently and that such a high proportion of current research is funded by commercial interests.

Here's one working definition of nature: biodiversity. That definition may not include, say, rocks—at least not directly—but it does describe the process: in order to survive, life needs other life, and it needs variety.

This is just as true in our homes, gardens, and urban neighborhoods as it is in the Amazon rain forest. When we think about the richness of our home environment, a useful analogy is the urban food desert: inner-city residents often have no nearby supermarkets; their choice of foods is limited to the most unhealthy foods, available in small convenience stores—if those stores are present. We also see park deserts. Urban neighborhoods limited to a handful of species are low on nutrition content—the nourishment to brain, body, and soul that comes from contact with species not our own.

On every level, human beings need the wealth of biodiversity. Similarly, rather than human monocultures—where everyone looks, consumes, produces, thinks, and votes alike—we need places of *human* diversity, where we live, work, learn, and play. A neighborhood or community with both high biodiversity and human diversity is a healthier community—a nature-rich city.

And that starts at home.

Make Good Use of What You Already Have

● **Go backyard camping, set up a patio tent, or create an observation blind.**
Buy or borrow a tent or encourage your kids to create their own tepee from a blanket, poles, or sticks. Leave it up all summer. Make s'mores, play flashlight tag, and make shadow puppets on the tent wall. Encourage them to run into the house for provisions from the refrigerator, and back out again. To turn the tent into a home-made observation blind, cut a small window in the side that faces a nearby bird feeder, bat house, or a place frequented by wildlife. Stow binoculars, field guides, a digital camera with a telephoto lens, water, and granola bars. Join the National Wildlife Federation's annual Great American Backyard Campout.

● **Experiment with rooftop camping.**
No yard? Before air-conditioning, pitching a hammock, dragging a mattress, or spreading a sleeping bag on a flat roof or fire escape was common. Rooftop camping, now on the rebound, is catching on with urban families and romantic couples. Pitch a tent. If it's windy, weigh it down with gear and face its opening away from the wind. Air mattresses: good idea. In Brooklyn, New York, a company called Bivouac arranges rooftop camping adventures.

It provides urban campers with artist-built lean-tos for rooftops, and requires that all electronics be left behind.

Hold a backyard picnic or tea party.

Kids can organize a backyard picnic with parents or by themselves. A blanket, some pillows, food and (optional) a pitcher of iced tea. If children are small, bring out a kettle and pour hot water over fresh mint or fresh lemon verbena. Or encourage the kids to make homemade lemonade. Bring a few nature books. And binoculars to watch the birds.

Get dirt!

Set aside a piece of ground in the backyard for kids to dig in. Research suggests that children strengthen their immune systems by playing in the dirt—and weaken those systems by avoiding dirt. In South Carolina, Norman McGee bought a pickup-truck-load of dirt and delivered it to his backyard for his kids to dig in. He reports that the dirt pile cost less than a video game and lasted far longer.

Mud is good. Put the garden hose to good use.

Then, on a hot summer day, add water. If you find critters in the mud, all the better. Or turn a dirt slope into a mudslide. All you need is a plastic tarpaulin, something to secure the corners, and some water. The British organization Play England publishes online instructions for making mudslides, mud piles, and—best of all—mud men. Wisdom from *Maria's Country Farm Kitchen*, a popular blog by Maria Rodale, chairman and CEO of Rodale, Inc.: "Kids walk in covered in mud? Don't freak out. Laugh about it and make them do their own laundry. Clothes are totally replaceable. Kids and nature are not."

Play with sticks.

In 2008, the stick was inducted into the National Toy Hall of Fame with this eloquent appraisal: "The stick may be the world's oldest toy." They can "turn into swords, magic wands, majorette batons, fishing poles, and light sabers . . . Children build with sticks, bat balls with them, and walk with them. They are the original building blocks for creative play." They also happen to be free.

Discover a hidden universe.

Find a scrap board and place it on bare dirt for a family experiment. Come back in a day or two, carefully lift the board (watch for unfriendly critters), and see how many species have found shelter there. Identify these creatures with the help of a field guide. Return to this universe once a week, lift the board, and discover who's new.

Go on a backyard bug hunt or plant safari.

Find camouflaged insects. Stick insects. Leaf bugs. Leaf bugs hitching a ride on stick insects. Look for spiderwebs early in the morning. Do an inventory of plant life; learn which plants in the backyard are native and which are not. Keep your eye out for any microbeasts that may be dwelling on or near the plants. Additional suggestions are offered by National Geographic.

Plot the "Escape of the Dolls."

Author Sara St. Antoine, who has studied the ability of children to create and tell stories, offers this suggestion: Move doll and action-figure play to the deck, yard, or park. Kids can turn tree stumps into houses, pinecones into furniture, and garden flowers into tropical jungles for their dolls. Later, children can tell or write stories about the outdoor adventures of their dolls and action figures.

Make a slug playground.

Get a small tray of cardboard, such as the bottom of a case of cat food or soup. Suggest to your kids that they make a miniature playground inside, using cardboard, sticks, paper, and toilet paper rolls to make slides, tunnels, seesaws, and more. They can put a slug, snail, or worm inside the playground and watch how it plays. Be patient. Very patient.

🌿 **Make a moth broth or wine rope.**

To make gooey moth broth, pour overripe "fruit, stale beer, or wine (or fruit juice that's been hanging around too long), and sweetener (honey, sugar, or molasses)" in a blender, suggests Deborah Churchman, in the journal *American Forests*. Go outside at sunset and spread the broth on a half-dozen trees. Come back with a flashlight when it's dark, and show kids the moths, ants, earwigs, and other insects the goo has lured. Or attract moths with "wine ropes." While heating a small amount of wine on the stove, mix in some sugar and keep stirring until the sugar dissolves. Dip thin lengths of cloth in the concoction. With your children, hang the strips from a tree branch outdoors at dusk, wait a couple of hours, and then return to see who showed up for the wine tasting.

🌿 **Make a backyard sun oven.**

If you live in a sunny place (and that moth broth made you hungry), your kids can cook marshmallows in a simple solar oven. Education.com suggests lining the inside of a large bowl with aluminum foil and setting it on a chair in direct sunlight, but not where animals can get to it. Then skewer a couple of marshmallows and set the skewer across the top of the bowl. After fifteen minutes, the marshmallows should be cooked. This goes well with chocolate and graham crackers.

BUILD A BACKYARD NATURE PRESERVE

Whether your available outdoor space is an apartment balcony, a suburban backyard, a rooftop garden, or a twenty-acre farm, you and your family can attract and support wildlife and help restore native habitat. The average cost for creating a habitat for butterflies and birds is $50 to $150 per seventy-five-square-foot plot, according to *Consumer Reports*; $10 if starting from seed. Animals need four things to survive—food, water, shelter, and places to raise their young. They need, in short, to be part of a healthy local food web, which includes creatures great and small, but begins with plants. Plants produce their own food through photosynthesis—combining carbon dioxide, water, and sunlight to produce sugar and oxygen. They serve, literally, as the root of all life. Recommended books: *Bringing Nature Home* and *Therapeutic Landscapes: An Evidence-Based Approach to Designing Healing Gardens and Restorative Outdoor Spaces.*

🌿 Take the biodiversity test.

Take inventory in your yard or other home green space. Better yet, ask your kids to draw up the list. "If you can only count five species of plants, including the lawn, you've got an overly homogenized landscape," says Damon Waitt, botanist at the Lady Bird Johnson Wildflower Center in Texas, as quoted in *Consumer Reports.*

🌿 Reduce your lawn, go native.

Lawns are now the largest irrigated crop in the United States. Replace all or part of your lawn—especially the areas that don't get much foot traffic—with bird-attracting plants, trees, and bushes, especially native plants. "Native" is not always easy to define, particularly as climate change begins to move species. But using native plants can produce yards that are beautiful, easier to maintain, and usually more drought-resistant. Even if you leave most of your traditional lawn in place, you can trim it with plants that enhance biodiversity and add to the appeal of your property. Many plant nurseries now offer native species, and nurseries that specialize in native plants have knowledgeable staff who can help find just the right plants for where you live, and offer tips on how to grow them. Check out the national Native Plant Nursery Directory. Also, the Lady Bird Johnson Wildflower Center has lists of recommended native plants by region and state.

🌿 Use as many woody plants as possible.

"Supplying birds with the caterpillars they need while nesting will bring just as many birds to your yard during spring and summer as a bird feeder does during winter," advises Doug Tallamy, chair of the Department of Entomology and Wildlife Ecology at the University of Delaware. As he points out, many folks have been taught from childhood that the only good insect is a dead insect, but the food web depends on native insects. "Food webs develop locally over thousands of generations, with each member of the web adapting to the particular traits of the other members of the web," he says. "Bottom line: if you want birds, or toads, or salamanders, or countless other species in your yard, you must also have plants that support local insects."

🍃 **Transform your yard, garden, roof, or window box into a butterfly rest stop.**
Help restore butterfly migration routes by planting seeds of indigenous pollinating plants that provide nectar, roosting, and food for caterpillars. Hollyhocks, for example, are host plants for the painted lady butterfly, lupine for the Karner blue butterfly, and milkweed for and honeysuckle for monarchs and other pollinators. Avoid planting butterfly bush (genus Buddleia), which is a good nectar plant, but does not support the larval development of any U.S. butterfly species. Position the flowering plants so they receive full sun from midmorning to midafternoon (butterflies prefer their nectar warm); make sure they have a place for "puddling" — wet sand or mud for drinking and gathering. See Audubon's guide for helping butterflies; the Butterfly Site, a database of host plants for butterflies and moths; and the North American Pollinator Protection Campaign. Purchase a sugar-water butterfly feeder, or make one out of a mason jar or baby-food jar with sealable lid, kitchen sponge, hammer and nail, and a saucepan. See Brightnest .com for instructions. Creating a butterfly rest stop is not only good for the environment; it also serves as a teaching and learning experience for kids.

🍃 **Recruit kids and other neighbors to help create the backyard nature preserve.**
Yards that don't attract insects are often the same yards that don't attract kids. But a nature-rich yard attracts both. Especially if kids, teenagers, and adults all take part in the planning and care

of the home nature preserve. When Palo Alto's Karen Harwell turned her six-hundred-square-foot backyard into a nature sanctuary with native plants, organic vegetables, ducks, a beehive, rabbits to pet, and calming places to sit and talk, neighborhood teens began to visit. It became their magical meeting place. Soon, families up and down the street caught the bug and began to transform their own yards.

🌿 Plant a sunflower pollinator garden and count the bees.

See pollination in action in your own pollinator garden. Plant a patch of annual sunflowers (the kind that grow, bloom, and die in one year) in a sunny spot. Plant biologist Susan J. Tweit offers this advice: "Don't use seeds for 'pollenless' flowers [varieties bred to be tidier and more saleable cut flowers]. Mark the location and note when the seeds sprout. Your kids can measure the sprouts as they grow, count how many buds each plant has, and when the flowers bloom, spend fifteen minutes every week counting how many and what kinds of bees visit your sunflower heads." Share observations and learn more about bees and other pollinators at the Great Sunflower Project.

🌿 Build a nature pond.

The National Wildlife Federation encourages people to establish backyard ponds to attract beneficial wildlife. Install a chlorine-free natural swimming pond cleaned by regeneration zones: aquatic plants, rocks, loose gravel, and friendly bacteria that act as water filters. Balanced backyard ponds rarely attract an unusual number of mosquitoes, according to NWF: "A variety of plants and animals will work together to maintain your pond as a healthy ecosystem."

🌿 Birdscape (or batscape) your property.

To create safer places for birds to make their nests, plant berry plants, thorny trees, and bushes. Hang a birdhouse and bird feeders. Commercial birdhouses are readily available, but AllCrafts.net has published fifty plans for DIY birdhouses, and they're free. You can also batscape your yard. Bat boxes are similar shelters for daytime bat roosting and can be made from scratch, too. For bat house buying guidance and DIY instructions, see the Organization for Bat Conservation or NWF's bat house guide.

Lose your marbles and make a bee watering bowl.

Fill a bowl or pie pan with marbles and sugar water, and set it outside. The bees will be able to perch on the marbles without falling into the water and potentially drowning. They'll convert the sugar into honey that will help the hive survive the winter.

With a few exceptions, don't feed wild animals.

Some naturalists make an exception for birds, bees, and butterflies, but overall, feeding wild animals isn't a good idea: it disturbs natural cycles, and can make wild mammals and larger predators too acclimated to human beings. That, in turn, can be dangerous to humans and their domestic animal companions. And keep cats indoors as much as possible, not only for their own safety, but because they take a huge toll on birds—studies show at least five hundred million a year in the United States—as well as lizards and other wild animals.

To learn more about backyard wildlife habitats, ask the experts.

For additional backyard suggestions, plus links to information about attracting wildlife to apartments and town houses, see the National Audubon Society's Invitation to a Healthy Yard. Your backyard may qualify as a National Wildlife Federation Certified Wildlife Habitat. Whether or not you certify your yard, you will gain useful information about growing native plants and supporting local wildlife. Also, the Cornell Ornithology Lab's Celebrate Urban Birds program offers resources about plants that grow well in containers and attract birds.

How a Jalapeño
Can Change a Life

· ·

We come to nature through different portals. I entered, as a boy, through the woods behind my house. Not so for Michael Pollan, author of *The Omnivore's Dilemma*, *Cooked*, and other books about our relationship with food and nature. When he was a boy, the woods made him nervous. So he came to nature through his garden. Later he would write, "The garden suggests there might be a place where we can meet nature halfway."

My friend Juan Martinez, who grew up in South Central Los Angeles, came to nature through a single chili plant. Juan grew up angry. "I was the poorest of the poor," he said. "People would make fun of me, people would tease me about my clothes. So it was my defense mechanism to pretty much kick their ass," he recalled. At the time, he seemed to be a prime candidate for a short, unremarkable gang life. When Juan was fifteen, a teacher gave him an ultimatum: Juan could flunk the class and be held back a grade, or he could join the school's Eco Club. Begrudgingly, Juan chose the club. "The first couple weeks, I didn't talk to people. I focused on growing my little jalapeño plant," he said.

He remembered how his mother had broken through a piece of concrete behind the family's house, exposing soil for a small garden. There, she grew jalapeños and medicinal plants, including aloe vera for cuts and burns. "She would make teas out of these plants whenever we were sick. So I wanted to show my mom that I could do that, too, that I could grow something, that I could give her something in return."

That entrance into the natural world changed Juan's life forever. Now thirty, he is a leader in the children and nature movement. Although Michael Pollan, Juan Martinez, and I came to nature from different directions, we arrived at the same destination.

THE YARD, BALCONY, OR ROOFTOP FARM

Not since the WW II Victory Gardens have so many families and individuals, with or without kids of their own, turned to their own land to supplement their diet. There's no need for a huge plot of land. A container on a patio or balcony, or a rooftop garden will do.

🌿 **Garden according to your age.**
Start small. Older folks have patience for the long garden view. But if your children are little, choose seeds large enough for them to handle and that mature quickly, like nasturtiums, peas, sunflowers, and beans. Keep chores manageable and don't try to do too much at once. Try to give kids ownership of a certain project or part of the garden. Suggested books: *The Book of Gardening Projects for Kids* and *Roots, Shoots, Buckets & Boots.*

🌿 **Create a high-rise garden.**
If you live in an urban neighborhood, a landing, deck, terrace, or flat roof typically can accommodate several large pots, and even trees can thrive in containers if given proper care. The pots can be a mix of food plants—tomato plants, for example—and decorative flowers, plants, and succulents. Recommended books: *The Edible Balcony* and *Balcony Gardening: A Beginners Guide to Starting a Beautiful Balcony Garden.*

🌿 **Plant the original fast food.**
That's the advice offered by *Maria's Farm Country Kitchen* blog. Strawberries, blueberries, or fruit can be eaten from the vine or branch. Even carrots, radishes, cherry tomatoes, or green beans can be pulled or plucked and then washed with a hose as instant treats right out of the garden, especially if the garden or pot is next to a play area.

🍃 Grow a pizza garden or a sunflower house.

Sharon Lovejoy's excellent books on gardening with kids, including *Roots, Shoots, Buckets & Boots,* contain multiple ideas for theme gardens that engage kids. Grow a pizza garden with your choice of ingredients—tomatoes, zucchini, peppers, spinach, onions, basil, oregano, and more—in the shape of a pizza. Grow a sunflower house by planting sunflowers in the shape of a playhouse. Plant a maze of flowers, or a moon garden full of flowers that bloom only at night.

🍃 Make seed bombs.

Combine a handful of soil, a small amount of water, and seeds of flowers native to your area. If the soil does not stick together and hold its form, add natural clay until it does. Make several of these seed bombs, let them dry until hard, then toss them where you want flowers to grow, especially in areas normally beyond reach. Recommended book: *This Book Was a Tree.*

🍃 Plant your socks.

Grow a sock garden. Find a pair of old socks you don't mind sacrificing, and let your kids wear them on a shoeless walk through a garden. Have them walk between plants—the socks will pick up seeds that would have been hard to see with the naked eye. Then, back at home, try to guess what kind of plants will grow when you plant the sock. For more instructions, see HowStuffWorks.com or Education.com. Or stuff a sock with compost, bury it, and wait to see what pops up in the spring.

🍃 Make a compost bin.

Composting is a rewarding family project that turns food and garden scraps into dirt that you use to grow food and ornamental plants in your yard or window box. One form of composting involves worms, which have "kid" written all over them. (Well, some kids.) Take turns turning the composter. This is a way to learn about the cycle of life. In nature, dirt doesn't come in bags. Recommended books: *The Complete Compost Gardening Guide* and *The Rodale Book of Composting.*

🌿 **Grow community in a garden.**
Especially important in urban neighborhoods, community gardens are trending. In San Francisco, for example, dozens of new urban farm and garden projects have been launched, and in 2011 the city changed its zoning code to permit urban agriculture in all neighborhoods. Created by neighborhood groups on both public and private land, community gardens bring people together. Some gardens sponsor seed and plant swaps and tool exchanges, and, of course, food. Online resources include the American Community Gardening Association, which publishes a list of current community gardens, and the Community Garden Start-Up Guide. Recommended book: *Community Gardens: Grow Your Own Vegetables and Herbs.*

🌿 **Share or sell the bounty.**
Through gardening, children and teenagers can help feed the family and the community. If your city or neighborhood has a farmers' market, your family may be able to sell extra produce there. Cultivate good relations with neighbors by sharing the food you grow, or donate food to a food bank.

🌿 **Head out to harvest.**
No land of your own? Families can spend a weekend picking berries, fruit, and vegetables on commercial farms or in orchards open to the public. Some local food co-ops invite the public to help with harvesting. Here are some ways to enhance your visit to a berry patch, and an easy recipe for refrigerator jam for your family, neighbors, friends, and relatives. And to find a pick-your-own farm near you (and to learn to can and freeze your picking), visit PickYourOwn.org.

🍃 **Raise chickens, ducks, goats, and other food-producing animals in your backyard.**

Hatch your own chicks from eggs, using an incubator (purchased or made at home), or buy day-old chicks from a feed store. Keep the chicks in a brooder (again, store bought or homemade). When they've grown, move them into an outside coop, giving each chicken approximately two to three square feet of space. If chickens don't strike your family's fancy, consider keeping ducks, for the eggs and the entertainment, and even goats. Municipalities are becoming more accommodating, reversing ordinances that excluded chickens and goats from the city. One backyard chicken rancher thinks of hens as "pets with benefits." See TheCityChicken.com and BackyardPoultry.com. Suggested book: *Backyard Livestock.*

🍃 **Install beehives.**

Although bee keeping is traditionally a rural hobby, it is becoming more popular in cities. Bees are crucial and threatened builders of a healthy ecosystem. If you're interested in starting your own backyard hive, check your local ordinances, talk it over with your neighbors first, find a bee club near you, and start attending meetings. Although you can buy bees in a package, it's worth investing in moderately more expensive "nucs," or nuclear hives, which are already-established hives that will grow into robust colonies much more quickly. Set up the hive in a spot close to a water source, not in direct sunlight. For more information, see BackyardBees.net, and Backyard Beekeeping for Beginners on the Mother Earth News website.

🍃 **Reduce hidden chemical risks in your yard and garden.**

Especially when kids are involved, herbicides, insecticides, and other pesticides pose real risks. Louise Chawla, a professor in the Environmental Design Program at the University of Colorado in Boulder, shares these and other suggestions: Plant an organic garden at home or in a neighborhood garden plot; practice organic lawn care with organic weed and insect treatments. "If you live in a homeowners association, build a coalition of other families with children and concerned neighbors to educate yourselves, the property manager, and board of directors about this subject," she adds. "Bring letters from your pediatricians about the importance of protection. Point out that safe lawns and gardens can be advertised as amenities that add to property values." For more information, see the Organic Land Care website and read Chawla's essay, "Child-Friendly Lawns and Gardens," at the Children & Nature Network website. Recommended book: *The Organic Lawn Care Manual.*

Map your own habitat.

"What does your yard look like from the perspective of a bird, a butterfly, or even a fox?" asks plant biologist Susan Tweit. She suggests mapping your own habitat, including trees, shrubs, flowers, water sources, and other features of your yard and garden. If you have a ravine behind your house or apartment building, add that, too. Besides being a great activity to do with kids, this map will help scientists understand how wildlife survives around people. Go to Cornell University's YardMap website, register, describe your location, and set up your site. Then go outside and begin collecting data on habitat. "It's easiest to start with the big features first: your house or any other buildings and 'hardscape' like driveways, fences, patios and sidewalks," according to Tweit. "Then note where the trees are (if there are trees), and then shrubs or hedges, and then flowers and other plants." Observe the kinds of birds and other wildlife that share your habitat. "Don't forget to map changes as well: when you plant new plants, or a tree dies, for instance."

How Family and Friends Can Help Create a Homegrown National Park

·······································

Kids, parents, and other adults can take a powerful next step by helping to create a Homegrown National Park. That's the dream of Doug Tallamy, whose book *Bringing Nature Home* I enthusiastically recommend. He makes the case that everyday gardeners are the key to reviving urban biodiversity—maybe global biodiversity. He argues that it is in the power of individual gardeners to make a difference to the future of the planet, to help reverse the biodiversity collapse. He points to worldwide data showing a one-to-one relationship between species loss and loss of native habitat. An example: In Delaware, 40 percent of all native plant species are threatened or extinct. And 41 percent of native birds that depend on native forest cover are rare or gone, according to Michael Rosenzweig, an evolutionary biologist based at the University of Arizona. Save a native plant; save a native bird.

Think of the power that kids would feel to be part of the regreening of a nation. Here's another possibility: Why not join with families and kids and others in other countries, to create a Worldwide Homegrown Park?

The notion is already taking root. The David Suzuki Foundation has created a homegrown park in Toronto. St. Louis, Missouri, has launched a Milkweeds for Monarchs initiative, through which the city has pledged to plant fifty monarch gardens and has challenged individuals and organizations to plant two hundred more. In Singapore, a Butterfly Trail near one of the main shopping areas not only attracts clouds of butterflies, but members of the Butterfly Circle, a group dedicated to observing and studying them.

In our cities, especially, the most effective thing we can do for biodiversity "is build biological corridors that connect isolated habitat fragments," says Tallamy. To do that will require a collective effort of all the landowners between the fragments, each person managing his or her property "as a living entity instead of an ornament." Some benefits will be immediate. People can look out their windows and be restored and rejuvenated. To illustrate the benefits his family receives, Tallamy sent me a photo. "Here's what my wife and I saw when we looked out at our garden fence yesterday." In the photo of his lush property, wild turkeys perched on a backyard fence.

Following his lead, my wife and I redid our yard, planting as many natives as possible. Animal species that we've never seen before are showing up, including native California butterflies and bees. The yard is beautiful. It doesn't require as much water. And it's low maintenance—I'll never mow again.

THE RESTORATIVE HOME: BRING THE OUTSIDE IN

Whether you are building a new house or retrofitting an existing home, here are a few tips to increase the restorative power of home. These ideas can also be applied to the workplace. Studies show that biophilic design—incorporating natural elements into the exterior and interior design of a building—improves psychological and physical health, creativity, and productivity. Interest in creating nature-rich indoor spaces is catching on, stimulated in part by the feng shui movement (arranging a living space for good *Qi*, or circulating life energy). Recommended books: *Biophilic Design: The Theory, Science, and Practice of Bringing Buildings to Life* and *Healing Spaces: The Science of Place and Well-Being.*

🍃 **If you can afford it, make sure you have a view of nature.**

Judith Heerwagen, environmental psychologist, advises her clients: "Most landscapes are designed to look good from the curb, but what you really want to do is create good views from inside."

🌿 **Design your home with the sun, wind, and other natural elements in mind.**

Place the house or arrange your furniture in sync with the sun's movements, so that sleeping and waking are in accord with available light; place large windows on the south-facing wall for passive solar heating, but also for a view of nature. Design for natural airflow with appropriately placed windows and high ceiling fans for natural ventilation. Combine solar panels with skylights. Install them over indoor plants and water gardens. Use lights that adjust throughout the day via sensors at the windows.

🌿 **Make space for indoor sit spots.**

Use indoor nature to create calming indoor places to sit, read, think, and meditate. Many hospitals now offer outdoor or indoor healing gardens for patients and their families. Workplaces are adopting the idea. Consider creating peaceful niches that are rich with nature, alive or symbolic. Biophilic elements do not always have to be living organisms. To augment real nature, biophilic or restorative architects incorporate the shapes and patterns of nature into the buildings and indoor spaces they design. Studies have shown that images of nature do calm us. A study conducted at a Swedish university hospital revealed that scenes of nature in artwork and murals reduced patients' anxiety and discomfort. We spend more time in our homes than in hospitals, so why not apply the nature principle to where we live?

🌿 **Create indoor gardens and living walls.**

In small apartments or large homes, create "living walls" of ficus, hibiscus, orchids, and other plants; or an indoor vertical vegetable garden with a drip-irrigation system. Such walls, first developed to improve air quality during space missions, can reduce indoor air pollution. In addition to carbon dioxide, plants can absorb many harmful chemicals such as benzene and formaldehyde through their respiration process. NASA recommends keeping one plant for every hundred square feet to maximize the benefits to indoor air. For lists of the most effective air-purifying plants, and for more information, see the websites Healthline.com or LivingInPerfectHarmony.com.

Decorate with natural materials, colors, textures.

Use nature-based furniture and decorations such as a dresser made of reclaimed wood, or floors or rugs made of sustainable bamboo or bamboo fabric. Use trees, living or dead, as decoration in high-ceilinged living rooms. Add nature's colors to your home in small ways, such as pillows, framed photos, candles, or dishware.

Use natural, recycled, and local building materials.

If site and regulations allow, build your home with cordwood masonry (lumber set in earthen mortar), cement mixed with recycled-paper pulp, aerated concrete, or straw-bale walls. Homes built with these materials can be so energy efficient that they need no air-conditioning. Whenever possible, use local materials to reflect the natural history of the region and deepen your sense of regional and personal identity.

Add therapeutic animals.

Dogs, cats, rabbits, and birds are employed in nursing homes and some schools to lower anxiety and increase the sense of well-being. Bird feeders and butterfly-attracting plants on ledges outside the window can also help. So can a view of a nature-rich yard, window box, or balcony.

Insulate for natural beauty.

Emphasize natural light and passive solar heating, as well as other green energy approaches. If your roof is slightly pitched, a green roof (essentially a garden on top of your house) can be installed by a certified contractor at about $13 to $45 per square foot. One method installs soilless growing material and mature plants able to withstand harsh weather. Your roof may need additional support. A green roof can last eighty years (compared with the forty-year average for conventional metal roofing or twenty-five years for asphalt shingles) and at the same time filter air and create habitat for migratory birds and butterflies, helping restore migration routes and your mental health. For more information, see the Green Roofs for Healthy Cities website.

Bring the sounds of nature indoors.

Purchase a good sound recorder, encourage your kids to record nature sounds, and fill your house with the sounds of nature. Some companies sell outdoor sound monitors for security but also to bring sounds of nature indoors. For example, the creators of Nature's Window offer a self-contained unit with indoor speakers and a "probe wire" that is passed through an open window that is gently closed on the wire, leading to outdoor sound monitors. An extended wire can be run to more distant nature features, such as a pond or trees that are visited more often by songbirds. Or, of course, you can open the windows. On especially cold or hot days, though, the device could be one way to bring nature's sounds indoors, and keep them there.

Warn the birds.

Across North America every year, as many as one hundred million birds are killed by collisions with windows. Birds just don't see glass. They see the reflection of trees, sky, and bird feeders in the glass, and house plants beyond the glass. Or they attack their own reflection, believing it's a predator. You can help by adding bird-warning elements to windows, such as ribbons, string, or mobiles. Or frost or etch the glass, or sponge or stamp decorative patterns on the windows, or cover the windows with CollidEscape perforated film to make windows visible to birds while still allowing people inside a clear view to the outside. Not only will the birds be safer, but you'll personally avoid the sadness that comes with the thunk. For more suggestions, see the Bird Conservation Network website.

BUY, BUILD, OR RENT A FAMILY GETAWAY CABIN

The family getaway cottage (or "camp" as they're called in the northern Midwest) is a longstanding but fading tradition in some parts of the world. But buying or renting a cabin in the woods or other natural area is still an option for some families. The biophilic design principles described above can also apply to that dream cottage in the woods.

🍃 **Tips for buying a cabin or cottage.**
To buy your own, it's best to work with a certified home inspector. The best time to cabin-hunt is in the spring, when winter damage is most evident. Check the quality of the electrical system and windows, how well the interior is sealed from outside elements, and whether floors are level. Look for signs of mold, and check the condition of the septic system (if it has one), winter road access, drainage, and slope (best is less than 10 percent and not more than 30 percent). You can recoup some of the cost by renting it to other families when you're not using it. Handle the details yourself, or seek out a property management agency that specializes in weekend rentals.

🍃 **Build your own cabin, with or without wheels.**
Buy the land; build the abode. Plans for building simple cabins are readily available. The small house or "tiny house" movement has caught on. Good books and other resources for buying or building your own cabin include: *Cabins: A Guide to Building Your Own Nature Retreat* and *Compact Cabins: Simple Living in 1000 Square Feet or Less*. By popular definition, a tiny house is 100–400 square feet (compared with the typical 2,400-square-foot American home). Some have wheels, making their footprint on wild land temporary. Though prefab tiny houses are available, most are custom built. For inspiration, see TinyHouseTalk.com. Still another option: houseboats.

🍃 **Rent a getaway cabin.**

For most families, a more realistic option is to find a timeshare or rental cabin, cottage, or houseboat. For far less than the price of a second mortgage, you can avoid debt and buyer's remorse. Pick a getaway place that your family can visit regularly, or try different cabins to experience a wider variety of natural areas.

A Cabin in the Woods

••••••••••••••••••••••••••••••••••

I n the 1980s, John Johns, a West Coast editor of airline magazines, was thriving. Then the parent company made him an offer he refused, because accepting the promotion would have required a move to the East Coast and away from his wife's extended family.

"So I bailed," he recalls. He worked for a while as a consultant and then, with no prior experience owning a business, he launched one. One weekend in the business's infant stage, he was visiting friends in the Tehachapi Mountains north of Los Angeles. "On a lark, we looked at cabins for sale. When we arrived at one of them, three deer were standing in the yard. A lightbulb went on. I thought: 'This is it.'"

But *it* made no sense. Going into debt for a cabin in the woods was not reasonable, especially with two kids in private school, a mortgage, and no foreseeable guaranteed income. Nonetheless, John and his wife, Dina, took a leap of faith. They bought the cabin. For the next decade, they took their young boys, Andrew and Christopher, to the cabin almost every available weekend.

"Sometimes the boys and I would go out and sit on a stump and just watch for deer, bobcats, quail," John recalls. "The boys usually hit the ground running, but during those quieter, more spiritual moments they barely moved. We just sat there and listened to the birds and absorbed it all. In the evenings, the whole family would sleep out on the deck and watch the stars."

The cabin gave the family a sense of grounding and renewal and wonder. "We grew up there. All of us." And the cabin shaped their future in an unexpected way. John grew his company there—in his mind. "Sometimes I went there alone, or with my business partner." Being there stimulated creativity and confidence. "I will always believe that our cabin in the woods fostered all the successes that followed. Family successes. Business successes."

John's company grew into a multimillion-dollar international corporation. Family ties strengthened. In fact, Andrew and Christopher never lost their love of nature. "Christopher and his girlfriend are rock climbers. They were on a cliff one day, suspended by a rope, and he turned to her and proposed," John says with a laugh. "Buying that cabin was the best investment I ever made."

Other Voices

"At home with my daughter, I sometimes bring a book with us into the woods. I set myself up, and she's free to roam and do what she wants as long as she's within shouting distance."
— *Kathee Krol, Pittsburgh, Pennsylvania*

"When I am engaged in nature, the kids around me are as well. I only interact with them if they initiate and I let nature do the rest."
— *Neill Bovaird,*
Wolf Tree Programs, Springfield, Massachusetts

"We have a back corner of our yard that is a bit overgrown. A tree with some big lilac bushes. I added some log 'chairs' and tuck a mirror and some shiny things in it too. We call it the 'Hidden Forest' though it's only a small area, fourteen feet by eight feet maybe, but giving it a name seems to inspire our five-year-old to play make-believe out there. Giving it bare outlines like log seats and mirrors means she can make it into a clubhouse, a fairy forest, or a tea party and opens up more possibilities. The area is frequented by birds and squirrels and even a fox once. We hang yarn out for nesting creatures to use."

—*Bianca Weeda, Denver, Colorado*

"I always give my daughter a corner of our family garden that's hers, exclusively. Her own trowel and gardening pouch in tow, she's set for hours, puttering, creating, and inventing imaginary stories. Mom gets to do her outdoor work unworried."

—*Natasha Bye, Durham, Ontario*

"In 1991, my wife, Marie, and I made a decision that would forever change our family for the better. Our daughters were ages three, five and seven. On a whim, we bought 60 acres of land just 30 miles southwest of Atlanta, with a collection of barns, a compact one-story historic farmhouse and a tiny tin roofed cottage. This was the beginning of a value shift that gently snuck up on us like a morning mist, when normal surroundings begin to look softer, calmer.

"My connection with my wife was magnified. Our date nights transitioned from social engagements to sharing a picnic with items harvested from the garden we tended as a family, and just talking—to each other.

"One evening at dinner, about four months after moving to the farm full-time, I asked the girls if they were happy with our decision. They looked at one another. I could tell they had talked about this. A united reply of, 'Yes, we love it' was delivered. I asked why.

" 'Because of the freedom,' they answered."

—*Steve Nygren, Serenbe, Georgia*

Part 4

······················

Nurturing Natural Resilience

*"Children still long to experience the freedom of the day:
I am convinced that the inclination survives, even if they
aren't given license to follow it. They want to confront the
world on their own terms. They want to discover what
'wild' means, and to find it for themselves."*
— ROBERT MICHAEL PYLE,
AUTHOR OF *THE THUNDER TREE*

*"Life isn't about waiting for the storm to pass . . . It's about
learning to dance in the rain."*
— VIVIAN GREENE, ARTIST

DON'T CUT DOWN THE TREE; BUILD UP THE KID

· ·

Every family wants comfort and safety. But as parents, we also want to raise courageous, resilient children and young adults—with a little help from nature.

The writer Robert Michael Pyle recalls his boyhood as "freedom of the day." Mistakes, scrapes, and discovery came with territory: "So what did it give me? Decisions; adaptations; discoveries; explorations. The ability to devise plans, and plan Bs."

One reaction to the fear in our society is to shut down; another is to turn the fear on its head, with the goal of building resilience.

Most broken bones related to tree climbing occur because the child doesn't have the strength to hold on to a limb, according to Joe Frost, professor emeritus at the University of Texas, Austin, and a leading expert on play and playgrounds. He recommends that parents work with their children to develop upper-body strength—early. "Doing so will significantly reduce the chance of serious injury."

So will taking small, manageable risks, which kids need to build their resilience.

"Too often, the focus is only on securing safer play materials, on setting rules and regulations, on substituting academics for playtime, and on neglecting the role of extensive play in child development," he says. Those approaches can result in "fragile, unskilled players, lacking judgment for avoiding injury." By contrast, play—physical, challenging play, the kind children often experience in natural settings—"builds brains, health, and fitter, safer children."

🍃 **Embrace natural resilience.**
Falling down is part of a well-balanced childhood. (And, for that matter, adulthood.) Children love exploring the dangers of nature—especially if there's a positive adult who helps them feel secure enough to take healthy risks, and if they fall, to learn to stand up again.

🍃 **Rather than banning all risk, make sure your child can manage the risk.**
Infants and toddlers require vigilant adults. "Oversight can be gradually relaxed as children develop strength, agility, and reasoning," says Joe Frost. It's also important to offer children appropriate risks that they can manage. For example, kids build their balancing skills by walking on logs. But when a log is too large, heavy, and unstable, it can exceed a very young child's ability to manage his or her own risk. Rather than eliminating all perceived risks, identify risks the child can manage—and provide nature experiences accordingly.

🍃 **Encourage frequent outdoor play to learn resilience skills.**
To develop skill in running, climbing, creating, assessing risks, and playing cooperatively with others, encourage children to play frequently, alone and in groups. This gives children time to find their own unique set of skills for engaging in safer play. "Dedicated, regular players develop intuitive skills that kick in very fast without conscious thought when facing possible injury," says Frost. "Observe experienced basketball players and climbers when they are falling or flopping. They intuitively turn onto the large flat portion of their backs, raise their heads to avoid contact, and avoid falling directly on fragile hands and arms."

🌿 Teach kids the fitness basics of outdoor play.

Tree-climbing instructor Tim Kovar urges climbers to follow a few simple rules, among them: make sure your tree of choice is living and strong; don't climb on branches smaller around than your wrist; always have at least three points of contact with the tree, meaning two feet and one hand, or two hands and one foot; and don't overreach for a branch—you can lose your balance. And, as mentioned earlier, to increase your child's safety, make sure she or he is continually building physical strength.

🌿 Associate nature with wonder and respect, not fear.

If a child's earliest relationship with nature is based in fear—fear of insects, snakes, imaginary tigers, natural disasters, fear of the ecological future—then that child will likely grow up associating nature with fear and destruction. Researcher David Sobel calls this contagious fear "ecophobia." On the other hand, fear can also be a source of fascination—if an adult sets the example for how to handle it.

🌿 Think in terms of comparative risk.

Yes, there are risks outdoors (though not nearly as many as the news media would have us believe), but there are huge psychological, physical, and spiritual risks in raising future generations under protective house arrest. Child obesity is just one of them. So, rather than giving in to those fears, we need to give our children the appropriate freedom they deserve. And we also have to come up with new, safe ways to get our young people and ourselves outdoors. Parents can't do this alone. Communities and organizations need to help.

🌿 Make sure kids have a variety of play environments.

Play and play environments should include spaces and opportunities for a wide range of play types—make-believe, group games, construction, rough and tumble, and interaction with the natural world of plant and animal life.

🍃 **Get the safety information you need about the natural world.**

Become familiar with useful resources for safety tips in the outdoors, including those with information on how to guard against ticks. One resource is the Centers for Disease Control. The website for the Audubon Society of Portland offers excellent general information on living with a variety of urban wildlife.

🍃 **Teach children to watch for behaviors more than just for strangers.**

That's the advice of family psychologist John Rosemond. Telling a child to stay away from strangers is relatively ineffective. "Stranger" is not a concept young children understand easily, he maintains. "Instead, children ought to be taught to be on the lookout for specific threatening behaviors and situations," he says. The National Crime Prevention Council website offers more information on helping kids determine who's a safe adult.

🍃 **Create a defensible nature-play space.**

Our sons also experienced nature in the urban canyon behind our house, building their forts, digging their holes, sitting under a tree coated with butterflies, all within our eyesight from our kitchen window. In 1972, architect and city planner Oscar Newman introduced the concept of defensible space, which he defined as "a residential environment whose physical characteristics—building layout and site plan—function to allow inhabitants themselves to become key agents in ensuring their security." This means being able to see where children are playing outside, from the edge of a park or from inside a home.

🍃 **More eyes on the parks and trails.**

Develop a walking/activity buddy system. Encourage kids to do nature activities together. With agreed-upon times and routes, kids, sometimes accompanied by parents, can meet up and walk together or bike together. Some young people are creating their own kids' nature clubs. Having more eyes on the parks, trails, and streets is a tried and true community policing principle. The more good people out there, the safer the outdoor areas will be.

Set geographic boundaries that expand through the years.

Setting physical neighborhood boundaries is a concept worth reviving. Parents should, of course, use their best judgment, based on the realities of their neighborhood and what they believe is age appropriate for their child. But children need boundaries that gradually open to the rest of the world to build judgment, trust, resilience, and to learn to independently recognize serious risk when they see it. It's the parent's job to set and enforce the boundaries; it's the growing child's job to stay within those boundaries or to ask the parent's permission to go beyond them, and to build trust.

Curiosity Conquers Fear

· ·

Many kids, particularly in urban neighborhoods, are afraid of nature, but that fear lifts when their curiosity is ignited.

"I teach inner-city preschoolers, and they're fascinated by anything natural," says Kathee Krol, who lives in Pittsburgh, Pennsylvania. "One day it was a fallen branch; another day it was the shredded bark from a tree. They collect acorns like squirrels preparing for winter. I have one girl to whom I showed seedpods, and she spent three days in a row this past week finding and then opening them and collecting what was inside."

But many teachers do report intense fear of nature among their students.

"I'm a public schoolteacher to urban kids," reports Diana Geer Marchant of Tuscaloosa, Alabama. "When I first started teaching in the outdoor classroom, the students were very reluctant to even go into the woods. I found that their fears of bears, bees, snakes, and other misconceptions were their biggest obstacle. I've been teaching them to respect and appreciate nature. I've taught them about the different animals and their place in the ecosystem." Now she sees her students taking the lessons and knowledge home. "They're exploring on their own and even teaching family members about what they've learned. So, for our students, making them feel safe and giving them knowledge was the first step to empowering them to explore nature."

Woodland Schoolhouse, a nature-focused school in Austin, Texas, takes its preschool class to the same forest and creek spots regularly. Teachers at the school find that young children more readily engage in deep, imaginative play when they are familiar with a space (versus being stimulated by a new environment). A teacher there writes, "It also allows me to relax and give them lots of space from the get-go because we're all familiar with the hazards and previously-agreed-upon boundaries of an area. They're checking in with me and testing boundaries less and focusing their energy on play with their peers."

BE A NATURAL NEIGHBOR

No one raises a child alone, including parents who believe they're alone. When it comes to connecting with nature, we all have different abilities and limitations: lack of prior experience, logistical and transportation challenges, time pressures, fear, physical and mental disabilities. By creating community, we can lower some of those barriers—and build new friendships for ourselves and our children at the same time.

🌿 **Identify neighbors you trust and ask them to help.**
One of the often-cited reasons for safety concerns is that as more parents entered the workforce, fewer were around to monitor children's play. But in some neighborhoods, that may be changing due to growing acceptance of flexible work hours and home offices, as well as a rising number of boomer retirees. Let trusted neighbors know your children's boundaries, including which natural areas are okay for the kids to visit, and ask them to call you if they see your child misbehaving or going beyond the boundary. You can do the same for other parents in the neighborhood.

🌿 **Create a Play Watch system.**
We have lifeguards for public swimming pools, so why not for urban nature areas? Several hours a week, parents—sitting on stoops, porches, or lawns at a respectable distance—can take turns watching neighborhood kids play. Parents can formalize that arrangement by creating a Play Watch system. The point would be twofold: 1) reduce danger to/crimes against kids; 2) raise awareness and give kids more freedom to play in neighborhoods and nearby nature. As part of the program, parents can create a communication plan, so that they know one another, the kids, phone numbers, and play and school schedules. They can also form neighborhood-based family nature clubs.

● **Encourage nature centers and schools to create gathering places for parents and other guardians.**

When the Cincinnati Nature Center built a large natural play space for kids—complete with a shallow stream, hills to roll down, places to dig—the staff made two unexpected discoveries about parent behavior. First, a deer fence created at the far edges of the play space not only kept the deer out, but gave parents a greater sense of security about letting their kids run loose. Second, when parents pointed out that there was no place for them to sit in the shade, the Nature Center built an open-sided shelter with picnic tables. Bill Hopple, the center's executive director, reports that both changes led to a dramatic increase in attendance. The shelter not only provided shade, but brought parents together socially to make new friends. And it helped parents stay at enough distance that children were more likely to play independently.

● **Join a nature organization that focuses on parent-child-community bonding.**

Strengthen parent/child and community relationships by participating in outdoor activities through YMCA Adventure Guides. Families can determine their level of involvement and participation in organized campouts and day-trips. Check with your local Y to find a group in your area. http://www.ymca.net/family-time

● **Kids can join nature clubs for kids sponsored by national and local organizations.**

Once upon a time, a young person could step outside the house and find someone to play with. Today, not so much. But parents can encourage their children to create or join nature clubs for kids. Scouting organizations and other formal groups are options. PBS's Dinosaur Train Nature Trackers Club describes itself as "a community of young children, their families and educators committed to learning about nature and doing good things for their environment." Print out the Nature Trackers Guide Book to get started. You can also print out a Nature Trackers Club sign "to mark your clubhouse!" In the UK, the Wildlife Trusts run more than two hundred nature clubs for children. These include Nature Tots and Wildlife Watch groups, junior volunteering groups, and WildPlay sessions for the whole family.

🍃 **Kids and young adults can create an informal nature club.**
Adult-organized groups are good options, but kids (perhaps with a little help from parents) can also form their own neighborhood or community clubs for kids and nature. Young people of college age can do this, too. For example, at the University of Alberta, in Edmonton, Canada, a group of students formed the Magpie Club to regularly escape the pressures of school by hiking in the nearby river valley. They do this both for physical exercise and for their mental health.

A BRIEF DEVELOPMENTAL GUIDE TO NATURE PLAY

Every child (like every adult) develops at his or her own pace, so drawing hard and fast rules about which nature activity is appropriate for each child is challenging. But here are some loose guidelines for age-appropriate activities in nature, and the parent's role. For a more complete developmental guide, see or download Nature Play & Learning Places by Robin Moore, professor of Landscape Architecture at North Carolina State University and director of the Natural Learning Initiative. Also see *Childhood and Nature: Design Principles for Educators* by David Sobel, founding director of the Center for Place-Based Education at Antioch University New England.

● **Recognize that infants need nature. Stay close by.**
Child-development researchers have only recently recognized the importance of outdoor involvement for babies in their first year. "For the crawling-learning-to-walk child, ground-level quality is critical," says Robin Moore. "Designated spaces can be small, intimate, enclosed with a gate, and have a simple layout." Assume that very young children are going to give unfamiliar objects the taste test, so be sure to remove potentially hazardous objects that can be mouthed.

● **Give toddlers loose parts and the space to explore.**
The early childhood years are a time for bonding with plants and animals through direct, even affectionate experiences as a part of learning and caring about others, according to David Sobel. Offer more chances for active exploration. Five-year-olds need to take charge of their nature experience. They need to be more daring, and they require more opportunities to solve problems on their own. This is also a good time to engage children in a backyard or community garden, so they can learn where food comes from.

● **Encourage kids in middle childhood to hunt, gather, and navigate.**
This period is what Sobel calls the "hunter-gatherer" age (though most of us carry that inclination throughout our lives). This is the time for collecting and classifying, and for more challenging activities such as building forts. The eight-to-eleven-year-olds need spaces large enough to feel "lost," says Moore. Spaces for young explorers might ideally include tree cover, bushes, and an area to build forts and other shelters of their own. At this point in their development, they need to learn to navigate the neighborhood and beyond.

● **Don't assume that preteens and teenagers no longer need nature.**
Some teens may prefer the mall to more natural habitats, but that does not necessarily mean they've lost interest in or no longer

need nature. As a later chapter will explore, nature provides young adults with rich opportunities to build personal identity, connections to other people, and social and environmental responsibility, and to explore potential nature-related careers.

LEAVE NO CHILD (OR ANYONE ELSE) INSIDE

I've worked with thousands of kids with disabilities and have seen, firsthand, the powerful effects that the world outside can offer them," says Kathy Ambrosini, a professional outdoor educator and the mother of a child with autism. She is also the originator of NatureAccess, a program begun in 1994 to ensure the inclusion of people with disabilities in outdoor activities and programming.

Accessible nature outings are all around us, she says. "Whether you're sharing the outdoors with an individual, family, social or school group, it's exciting to watch these kids develop new coping strategies and shake loose the grip of their symptoms while they enjoy, explore, play and connect in nature."

For parents, teachers, and outdoor programs, Ambrosini offers the following tips, which can apply to children and adults with just about any set of abilities. More ideas can be found at the National Center for Accessibility website. Recommended books: *Making Outdoor Programs Accessible* and *Smart Moves: Why Learning Is Not All in Your Head.*

🍃 **Consider different approaches to mobility.**

If a physical disability limits a child's mobility, try a jogging stroller with knobby tires for a comfortable ride over sand, roots, or rocks along trails. There are some excellent all-terrain wheelchairs on the market, some of which can be found at parks and preserves for loan. Inquire ahead or contact a local independent living center for suggestions of where these may be available. Among the many sources for all-terrain wheelchairs and other new outdoor mobility aids are Innovation in Motion (Mobility-USA.com) and My Special World (MySpecialWorld.net).

🍃 If they're young and anxious about going outside, bring along something or someone familiar and comforting.

Follow Ambrosini's example and host Teddy Bear Adventures: each child brings a favorite stuffed animal for a shared experience in nature. Or encourage children to invite friends or families, with or without disabilities, to help boost confidence and build social skills. She also recommends that families start hiking clubs to increase social opportunities. "Without these shared experiences, how will they build important social relationships?"

🍃 For children ages four and up, technology can be a supportive tool.

Smartphones, digital cameras, and binoculars are good filters for kids with attention disorders. They help a child focus on a single feature and reduce overloading visual stimulation. Digital technology can also provide a way for some people with disabilities to explore nature and then make the transition back indoors. For example, Ambrosini encourages the use of a digital recorder to capture bird songs and other pleasing sounds along the trail. "When they're back indoors, they can then use these recordings to calm themselves and reduce their anxiety." That's a good idea for all kids.

🍃 Optimize the kinesthetic.

"Think of an outing as a kinesthetic experience, where the children are on the move in active pursuit of something: reaching the tree at the top of the hill or scavenging for some new discovery along the trail," Ambrosini advises. "And once you're out exploring nature with children, you'll realize that you're feeling better, too!"

"My Feet, Six Inches from the Ground"

Bill Stothers, a retired journalist and disability activist for sixty years, describes his connection to nature, then and now, and the need for more awareness of accessible nature connections: "When I went out, someone pushed me in my wheelchair. My feet stayed put, about six inches off the grass, the sidewalk, the gravel roads. The natural world seemed to slip away, vibrancy fading out of touch. As I became older, I took up photography and found myself spending lots of time in local parks, getting close to and making pictures of flowers, plants, and outdoor life. That anxious feeling ebbed.

"Due to the efforts of people with disabilities, national, state and local parks are providing accessible trails and features that make it possible to get closer to flowers, trees and even animals—without paving paradise. And people with disabilities are more active than ever in outdoor sports, recreation and games. Organizations such as Easter Seals (and many local and regional groups) offer more organized activities, from summer camp and sports. But I fear too few kids with disabilities get much unregulated, unorganized time in the natural world. They love to touch the wonders of the earth, getting dirty in the grass, trying to grab a lizard or a worm or a bug. I still do, too.

"As time has passed, I have kept up my picture-making and it helps me connect with the real world around me. My feet continue to skim six inches above the grass. Still, I can stick my nose closer to the roses in my front yard and take in the perfume. I can rub my hands over the bark on the big tree in my backyard. And even though the techs tell me not to, I can't stop powering through puddles. Splashing and grinning."

CALL IN THE REINFORCEMENTS: GRAND IDEAS FOR GRANDPARENTS & GRANDFRIENDS

Grandparents and grandfriends (that's what children and nature advocate Avery Cleary calls older people who act as surrogate grandparents) can play an important role in connecting children to nature. They often have more free time, or at least more flexibility, than parents do. Also, many grandparents (one in ten in the United States) are raising a grandchild, according to a Pew Research analysis.

Grandparents and grandfriends seem younger these days. Many are, certainly in spirit. But sometimes the new sixty-five is, well, the new sixty-four.

So health is on the mind. Here's some good news: a growing body of scientific evidence links healthy aging to outdoor experiences, which add value to exercise, improving sleeping patterns, speeding recovery from injuries, reducing pain, and helping maintain brain function and memory. Residential developers already know that retiring baby boomers appear to prefer hiking trails to golf courses. Later, when choosing a long-term care facility, picking one with more nature in and around it helps (and some are taking biophilic design seriously).

All of this helps us age more gracefully, but nothing rejuvenates many of us quite so much as connecting the young to nature, through our families, volunteer programs at parks, religious or service organizations, and conservation groups. Not only do kids quicken the pulse, but they offer immeasurable ingredients to health and happiness: social contact, meaning, the infusion of wonder, to kids and adults, of every age.

🌿 Keep it simple, especially at first.

Barbara R. Duncan says she takes her three-year-old grandson outside to "do small things . . . that capture his attention, like picking up rocks . . . and feeding the ducks." Jeffrey Willius advised,

"It's the very simplicity that stymies some folks. My own grandpa would plop me down on the lawn, turn on the hose, and have me watch for night crawlers to be flooded out of their burrows. Then we'd go fishing." A twofer.

Create a grand garden.

"From an early age, I remember being in the garden with my grandparents," writes Penny Ellis Maurer, "weeding, watering, learning . . . Then the fruits of our labor were brought into the kitchen where I learned the finer points of canning, preserving and preparation from my grandmothers. It's the joy of sharing it with someone that makes it special."

Pack a Grand G.O. Bag.

Marti Erickson stashes two or more daypacks in her trunk, filled with binoculars, extra jackets, and nature guides for sudden getaways with her granddaughter. She also makes a practice of keeping two collapsible chairs in her car trunk. If she's having a particularly stressful day, she drives to the closest patch of nature, sits on one of those chairs, and is soothed. "My oldest grandchild likes nature breaks, too, and joins me when we're out together."

Tell the grandkids about your own childhood nature adventures.

That time you saw a mountain lion, the fish that got away, your own three-story tree house. Ni Ke, a mother who lives in Tonga, describes how her eighty-four-year-old mother "tells her grandchildren the songs they sang" in hard times, and the simple skills they learned, including "how to make garlands and how to keep pressed flowers." Ni Ke's father told his grandkids "about riding from his village in the mountains in Cyprus on a donkey to help work the fields," and he taught his grandkids how to cook outside. In addition to relating stories orally, grandparents can make a video or audio recording or write and share stories about their experiences.

🌿 Purchase a senior park pass.

State and national parks and national wildlife refuges are eager to see you. In fact, the National Park Service offers a lifetime pass (currently a $10 onetime fee) to people age sixty-two and older. That's a deal, especially if you're entering a park by car with children under sixteen. They get in free, too.

🌿 Grandparents and grandchildren can learn a new outdoor skill together.

It's never too late to learn to camp or hike. Take a tracking course together. Sign on with a dinosaur dig. Ni Ke's sister, age fifty-eight, recently "learned to ride a bike herself" alongside her four-year-old granddaughter. "That's something they did together." (Interesting factoid: today, because fewer people learned to ride bikes when they were kids, REI is providing bike-riding classes for adults.) Ask your grandchild about snowboarding. Be brave.

🌿 Start a grandparents group.

Join or start a Grandparents or Grandfriends Nature Circle to overcome your own nature-deficit disorder. A Nature Circle is similar to a support group, but more fun and without the whining.

🌿 Invite the grandkids over for a backyard campout.

You'll not only be helping your grandkids; you'll be giving their parents some private time to spend as a couple.

🌿 Respect family boundaries.

A cautionary note about family dynamics: depending on the situation, grandparents should take care to offer nature experiences in a way that supports parents. Multigenerational outings of the whole family often work best. You're the mentor, not the boss.

🌿 Pass nature forward.

Boomers could be the last generation to remember a time when it was considered normal and expected for children to play in the woods and fields. When we leave this earth, will the memory of such experiences leave with us? Reconnecting the young to the natural world (as we reconnect ourselves) could be our greatest, most redemptive cause.

THE HUMMINGBIRD PARENT

Every responsible parent is, and should be, concerned about the risks his or her children take—including risks in nature. But sometimes parenting advice can go to extremes. Some experts sternly warn parents about all the dangers, real or assumed—from strangers to noxious weeds—lurking outside the front door. At the same time, parents sometimes find themselves shamed for their fear.

"With all of the talk about giving kids leverage and freedom from a very early age, you start to feel guilty when you help your kids," writes guest blogger Michele Whiteaker in *The Grass Stain Guru*, a blog by Bethe Almeras.

"I hate to admit it, but fear and anxiety are definitely factors," she writes. It's hard not to be consumed by that fear, given the horrendous reality of crimes against children. Yes, it's true that the number of abductions and child murders has been decreasing in recent years, and our perception of danger is greatly amplified by media hype. But parental fear is real. It should be respected, not dismissed. Even with this fear, most of us want to make sure our children have as much independent play as possible for their healthy development, including play in the natural world.

"In the range from helicopter to neglect—I probably fall a bit more toward helicopter," adds Whiteaker. She's referring to the term helicopter parent, often used in a pejorative way to describe overprotective parents. "In fact, I call myself a hummingbird parent. I tend to stay physically distant to let them explore and problem solve, but zoom in at moments when safety is an issue (which isn't very often)."

Notice that she isn't hovering over her kids with nature flash cards. She stands back and makes space for independent nature play—albeit not as free as she experienced as a child. This play is important nonetheless. "Common sense needs to rule on this issue," she adds. "Are helicopter parents bad for caring so deeply about their kids? Certainly not. Will their children be scarred for life? No. Should parents back off and let their kids take reasonable risks? Yes!"

So, thinking about this after I first quoted Whiteaker and cited her idea back in 2010, I suggested a way to further define the concept:

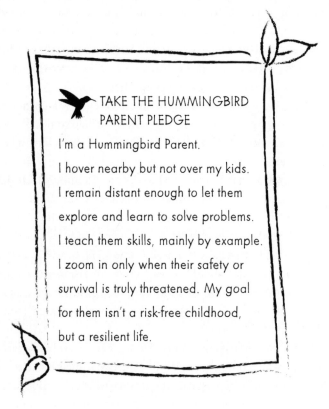

TAKE THE HUMMINGBIRD PARENT PLEDGE

I'm a Hummingbird Parent.

I hover nearby but not over my kids.

I remain distant enough to let them explore and learn to solve problems.

I teach them skills, mainly by example.

I zoom in only when their safety or survival is truly threatened. My goal for them isn't a risk-free childhood, but a resilient life.

Other Voices

"I sent my kids outside with the suggestion that they 'go look for an adventure.' The rest was up to them. When they came back in, I would ask them to describe their adventures. They had days and days of playing out a story. Andy and his friend Craig played pirates, Davy Crockett, and fighter pilots. Cindy and her friend Michael played Tasmanian Devils, Traveling Rock Band, and Robinson Crusoe. They built forts, cabins, trails, camps, and tents, in the chaparral on our property and the friends' property. They slept out on the lawn in the tents. There were real adventures such as spotting a bobcat. Nothing terrible happened. Now I have a new baby granddaughter. When she was two days old, we took her outside to look at the wisteria and the bougainvillea. I'm looking forward to sharing her adventures!"

— *Linda Corey, San Diego, California*

"The best step parents can make is that first step off the doorstep. It's not kids who need encouragement, it's parents."

— *Conor O'Gorman, Chester, UK, OutdoorsWithDad.org*

"Dogs help inspire exploration; they actually build confidence in children and point out things to the kids."

— *Degania Fortson, Landstuhl, Germany*

"Send them out together with a protective dog! I have no children, but when I was young, I went out into the woods to dance like a ballerina in a small spotlight of sunbeams between the trees (yeah, really! Such a romantic little princess I was). Now, as a grown-up, I work as a wildlife journalist, writing about what we can learn from nature. I think a lot of my creativity was developed while I was alone, with nature as my playground."

— *Lucienne van Ek, Amsterdam, The Netherlands*

"Take them to the same forest often. Let them get comfortable with the space. Set up a 'home base' with a blanket. Then tell them to 'go play.' Depending on the age of the child, tell them they can only go as far as they can still hear you. You can even create a little call and response like birds do: using any two word or sound combination. Then every five minutes or so you can make your 'call' and they can make their 'response.'"

—Jessica Clayton, Brick Township, New Jersey

"Thinking about this brought to mind me and my grandson walking/riding scooters to the library last year. My grandson fell down, and instead of crying, began naming and talking about the insects he saw as he was lying on the ground!"

—Dennis W. Schvedja, North Haledon, New Jersey

"When I was little, my mom let me walk, alone, about a mile and a half down to the creek. And that has made, as Mr. Frost said, all the difference."

—Catherine Giovannoni, Arlington, Virginia

Part 5

Go Wild
and Wilder

"You can't know who you are until you know where you are."
— WENDELL BERRY

THE WILD NEARBY

· ·

Experiencing the wild can begin close to home, in your own neighborhood and bioregion. But sometimes wildness can be all around you and you don't even see it.

I came to San Diego directly out of college in Kansas. For years, I had a difficult time attaching to this strange new land. I was place-blind. One reason was that Southern California lacked the rooted familiarity of the landscape of my youth. Another reason, perhaps, was that I did not trust that the nature of San Diego's urban canyons or the wildness of its backcountry, always threatened by development, would last long enough to warrant my investing it with my love. So I had no clue how nature-rich my adopted corner of the world was, until, as a journalist, I made it my job to dig deeper.

A bioregion is a geographic area defined less by human history than by natural history; it has its own natural topographic and biological borders. Now, I realize that my home, though one of the most densely human-populated bioregions in the United States, also includes the most biodiversity of any county in the country. This is a hot zone of animal and plant life, a land of microclimates, of ring-tailed cats and mountain lions, condors, whales, sea turtles, great white sharks, waterspouts, and firestorms. In Northern Baja California, also part of this bioregion, isolated sky islands jut above the clouds; there, life remains "a relic of the Pleistocene," as one biologist describes it, "Ethereal . . . primeval."

This strange, otherworldly land has nurtured my family. To my sons, this is home. It's part of who they are.

Explore Nearby Nature

🍃 **Find nearby nature by exploring your own neighborhood.**

Inner-City Outings is a Sierra Club–sponsored volunteer program that organizes people in inner-city neighborhoods. On their first outing, young people, with backpacks, take a five-mile hike in their own neighborhood in order to identify patches of nearby nature — parks, back alleys, gardens, vacant lots. Your family can also join a nature center or a local branch of Audubon or the Sierra Club.

🍃 **Go online to find nearby nature.**

Go to the Nature Conservancy's online guide, located at NatureRocks.org, tap in your ZIP Code, and find opportunities for nature time near your home, including parks, lakes, campgrounds, and so forth. Another good resource for finding nature on public lands near your home is DiscoverTheForest.org. To find a walking, hiking, or biking trail near you, visit TrailLink.com, sponsored by the Rails-to-Trails Conservancy. Some of the trails listed and described are on converted rail lines, others are not, but there's sure to be one near your home.

🍃 **Respect the lost urban islands of nature.**

That cluster of trees at the end of the cul-de-sac, the ravine behind the housing tract, the green urban alley, even the cracks in a sidewalk, nurture life. They may not be biologically diverse, but for children they can be the doorways to a parallel universe. "These are places of initiation, where the borders between ourselves and other creatures break down," writes Robert Michael Pyle, "where the earth gets under our nails and a sense of place gets under our skin."

🌿 **Look for the edges.**

Even if an urban or suburban park is flat turf frequented mainly by soccer teams, wildlife often thrives at the edges. In fact, when the soccer balls aren't flying, you'll often see kids and adults playing at or exploring the edges where the turf ends and the weeds and rocks begin. Biologically, the most complex communities of life always live at the edges, where one ecological zone ends and another begins.

🌿 **Discover and adopt a great urban park.**

When we look for nature, with images of wilderness in our minds, we often overlook our great urban parks. Rediscovering them can open new worlds. "We dubbed our favorite spot... 'The Milkweed Field,' writes Lauren Knight in the *Washington Post*. "It was on the edge of Rock Creek Park, not far from a very busy road, but set far enough back to be out of eye- and earshot of the traffic. In the summer, the field grew tall and green, with deer trails throughout. In the fall, hundreds of milkweed pods exploded with fluffy white seeds and we marveled at the monarch butterflies that congregated near the plants on their migration south. This place was magical, and right in the middle of the city."

🌿 **Go on an old-fashioned picnic in the park.**

This is something of a lost art. Families of recent immigrants are often more likely to go on a picnic or have large group gatherings outdoors. Park rangers who have watched visitations dwindle are especially appreciative of this. A picnic in a park is also a way for families with members with disabilities to connect with nature. Eating outdoors is fairly straightforward but does pose some adaptive challenges. The website DisabledTravelAdvice.co.uk offers a guide for making picnics more accessible.

The Special Place

······································

The late, great Brother Yusuf Burgess, one of the most inspiring leaders of the children and nature movement, often spoke of his special place in nature:

"My mother made sure I often escaped the crowded projects by visiting Brooklyn's Prospect Park. By nine years old, I could get there alone by bus or subway. I would wander the park, identifying trees, catching bumblebees in jelly jars, and filling paper cups with tadpoles to raise at home. In the park was a favorite tree I'd climb and get lost in the canopy, unseen by the rest of world. This was my place to daydream, relax, or travel anywhere I'd read about in my 'Weekly Reader.' It's the 'Place' I can, even now, return to at any moment when I am stressed or need to meditate and rest."

As a seventeen-year-old, Yusuf served in Vietnam; later he suffered from drug and alcohol addiction. He credited his recovery to the foundation provided, in part, by his early experiences in Prospect Park, and to a wise counselor, who prescribed kayaking in wilderness areas. A recipient of the Andrew Goodman Foundation Hidden Heroes Award, Brother Yusuf dedicated the rest of his life to connecting urban youths to nature, in Albany, New York, and around the world.

Bond with Your Bioregion

🍃 **Make a mental map of your bioregion.**

Learn about your bioregion the old-fashioned way: from local guidebooks and regional nature field guides. Some offer detailed descriptions, maps, levels of difficulty, and age-appropriate suggestions for activities and hikes. In some regions, you can buy topo maps, which reveal the lay of the land and watersheds of your region. Apps are also available for urban and regional hiking trails.

🍃 **Join a group that explores a sense of place.**

Exploring a Sense of Place, launched in 2001, organizes group outings, led by local nature experts, in several bioregions around the United States, and offers leadership training and local courses. ESP also publishes a guidebook. Close to Home, a San Francisco Bay Area effort, organizes monthly talks and field trips. The organizers of Close to Home explain their purpose by quoting the great nature photographer Galen Rowell, who confessed in his book, *Bay Area Wild*: "Though I had spent decades celebrating the grand design of natural areas around the world in words and photographs, I had looked right past the extraordinarily rich and varied wild hills, valleys, delta, bay, ocean, islands and mountains in my own backyard."

🍃 **Drive less, walk and run more—and use your "learning machine."**

Bikes are increasingly seen as an alternative to driving cars. Walkable-city advocate Dan Burden describes his bicycle as the "learning machine." "With the bike, and later my feet," he says, "I began to explore everything rural, everything urban, to appreciate what made each unique and distinct." On a bike, he adds, "You go at nature-speed."

"Parks Are for People Who Look Like Me"

....

Rue Mapp is founder of Outdoor Afro, a community of African American adults and families connecting with nature and each other. It uses social media to connect people to events and to meet up with one another for outdoor recreation and personal enrichment. She's also a proponent of *creating* nature in urban places, even if the creation is symbolic.

Pop-up parks, or "parklets," are temporary landscapes, usually in parking lanes. People bring potted plants and other greenery and mark off the borrowed territory for adult socializing and kids' play. The notion originated in the pavement-to-parks movement in New York and San Francisco.

"It's a drop-in experience," says Mapp. "Neighbors bring barbecue cookers, offer salsa lessons, hold a birthday party. Commercial food trucks often roll up. Pop-up communities form." Pop-up parks aren't organized by the Parks Department or necessarily blessed by an elected official, but they're something people need. "We're no longer waiting for permission; we're just doing it."

Another approach comes from Marielle Anzelone, a botanist and urban ecologist who wanted to remind people of the importance of nearby nature in New York City. Blending botany with art, Anzelone and her team raised more than $25,000 on Kickstarter to create PopUP Forest: Times Square, a large, temporary nature installation of trees, native wildflowers, and soil, to be hauled into "the most unnatural place in the world."

In addition to providing three weeks of green relief for Times Square, the goal was to highlight the remaining natural areas of New York that need protection. "Nature gets so little attention, but biodiversity loss is at the same crisis level as climate change," she told *Grist* magazine. "I want to get people's attention—and what's one way to get attention? Grabbing public space, and setting up a forest in the most incongruous place imaginable." Anzelone hoped to redistribute pieces of the pop-up forest to local parks and schoolyards.

Mapp is a champion of big parks, too. Only about one in five national park visitors is nonwhite, according to a 2011 report commissioned by the National Park Service. Only about one in ten is Hispanic. "It's my goal to help generate a future where people of every hue know that not only public plazas, but also parks and wild spaces are their inheritance, and theirs to benefit from and support," she says. "Parks are for people who look like me."

Several groups in addition to Outdoor Afro are working toward the same goal, and they invite your participation. Among them are American Latino Expeditions and GirlTrek. The recreation retailer REI is teaming up with the National Park Foundation to address the issue. In addition to checking out the organizations above, see these blogs: *GirlGoneTravel* and *Traveling Latina*.

BECOME A CITIZEN NATURALIST

Nothing builds love of nature like taking care of it. Around the world, the new nature movement is encouraging people of all ages to become citizen naturalists—sometimes called citizen scientists, amateurs who combine work and play to understand and protect nature close to home, and then the farther wilderness. Citizen naturalists are becoming increasingly sophisticated.

🍃 **Families and young adults can volunteer at local nature centers, nature preserves, and parks.**
Some nature centers offer so-called junior ranger programs to young people, ages thirteen to seventeen, to teach outdoor leadership, mountaineering, rescue skills, wilderness survival skills, and train young citizen naturalists. Look into volunteer opportunities at a botanical garden or local park.

🍃 **Help remove invasive plant species from your community and bioregion.**

Commander Ben (Benjamin Shrader) is a sixteen-year-old who visits public schools across Texas to teach younger kids about invasive plant species and how to fight them. Ben writes a terrific blog, at CommanderBen.com, and makes videos about his war on invasive plants, which he posts on his YouTube page. For general information, see the website for the National Invasive Species Information Center, which offers a map of programs by state.

🍃 **Join a Master Naturalist community.**

Join one of the regionally based Master Naturalist groups. For example, the California Naturalist Program, part of the University of California Cooperative Extension, helps train volunteer naturalists and citizen scientists to take active roles in conservation, education, and restoration. In addition to its adult membership courses, California Naturalist currently offers a one-week youth immersion course for high school students. Look for similar opportunities in your own region.

🍃 **Learn about phenology. That's right, phenology.**

Phenology is the study of timing events in the lives of plants and animals, and how behavior and physiology are influenced by variations in seasons and climates—an especially valuable skill in the age of climate change. Network participants worldwide upload their findings. At the same time each year (spring is best), observe nature near where you live. Is one kind of tree budding before the others? What's the first migratory bird that you spot? Record as many similar observations as possible and compare results from year to year to see if any patterns emerge. Resource: the USA National Phenology Network, which offers an excellent, clearly written botany primer.

Be a science scout.
Help scientists track everything from meteors, to mountain lions, to blue catfish — even sharks. SciStarter and California Academy of Science are two great websites that list opportunities to help scientists understand the natural world, including ones you can do in your own neighborhood or backyard.

Be a bird counter.
The Cornell Lab of Ornithology invites the public to join the Celebrate Urban Birds project, with kits in Spanish and English. Participants in the project are encouraged to garden, create nature-related art, and observe neighborhood birds, then send the data online to scientists at the Cornell Lab. The project focuses on species of birds often found in urban neighborhoods. Also from Cornell Lab, BirdSleuth.org provides resources for kids K–12, and FeederWatch.org (information on the Cornell Lab website) helps them protect species by contributing a seasonal tally. At Birdpost .com, young people can post their bird sightings onto satellite maps and track bird populations in their own neighborhoods. Participate in the Great Backyard Bird Count.

Monitor monarchs.
Monarch Watch is a University of Kansas educational outreach program that involves schoolchildren and other nonscience professionals in collecting data used in the study of monarch butterfly migration and the conservation of the monarch habitat. Students can compare the timing of monarch butterfly migration in their area with that in other regions. Journey North gives students the opportunity to monitor the northward progression of spring throughout North America by gathering and exchanging data on wildlife migration, the budding of plants, changes in light levels, and other seasonal events.

🌿 **Be a bird, goat, lion, or ant counter.**
As mentioned earlier, the Cornell Lab of Ornithology sponsors the Great Backyard Bird Count. But birds aren't the only animals that count. The Anza Borrego Desert Park has, in the past, organized citizen naturalists into counting teams for mountain goats. The Bay Area Ant Survey recruits citizen naturalists to help document more than a hundred distinct types of ant species in the eleven-county Bay Area.

🌿 **Do water testing and other types of watershed monitoring.**
Many government agencies and other organizations have local monitoring projects in which school classes can become involved. For example, the Missouri Stream Team provides training for citizens so that they can effectively monitor streams and solve stream problems in their area. Participation in the program gives students opportunities to observe seasonal changes affecting the macroinvertebrates (organisms large enough to be seen with the naked eye and lacking a backbone) in streams.

🌿 **Adopt and nurture a piece of the earth.**
Pick a natural area in your neighborhood or city and become its caretaker—pick up litter, plant trees and shrubs, hang bird feeders, or water plants. Maybe it's already your "sit spot." You may be amazed at how much your relationship with the natural world changes when you have stewardship over even a small part of it.

🌿 **Put your money where your ideals are.**
Follow the lead of the great conservationist Aldo Leopold. Buy a piece of worn-out agricultural or industrial land, preferably in a wildlife corridor, remove junk and invasive species, plant native species, encourage native wildlife. Love it to life.

🌿 **Be a plant salvager.**
The Native Plant Salvage Program, run by the King County Department of Water in Washington State, has "saved tens of

thousands of plants in the path of commercial and residential development" by enlisting hundreds of volunteers—adults, kids, and young people—to transplant them. Get there before the bulldozers do.

🍃 **Help restore habitat on land or in water.**
Restore damaged habitat and monitor rare and endangered species. An array of opportunities, some of them in ecotourism, exist. You and your family can get involved through natural history museums, state and national parks, and wildlife protection groups. Example programs include the Tucson Succulent Society and the Wild Ones. Or "embrace a stream," as Trout Unlimited calls stream reclamation.

Every Kid in a Park

·····································

I n September 2015, a new White House initiative called Every Kid in a Park went into effect. It's an ambitious plan to provide all fourth grade students and their families with free admission to our national parks and other federal lands and waters. A surprising number of these special places are in urban areas.

This won't be a one-time-only pass. Children, their families, adult chaperones, and their schools will be able to use the pass for multiple visits over the course of an entire year. These passes are accessible and distributed to fourth graders and their families through schools and youth organizations.

Supporters of the initiative are working to raise millions of dollars from private and corporate contributions to finance school trip transportation and to engage educators and parents. If Every Kid in a Park thrives in coming years, an entire generation of children will have visited the parks—some of them more than once. These kids might otherwise never set foot in a national park or other federal natural lands.

"Fewer than half of all kids in the United States can safely walk to a park from their home," according to Jackie Ostfeld, who cites a CDC statistic. She is cofounding chair of the Outdoors Alliance for Kids, one of the many organizations, including the Children & Nature Network, to support the initiative.

National Parks Director Jon Jarvis is especially excited about the potential of using the trips to encourage schools to incorporate more nature studies into their curricula and to recognize research that suggests there is improved cognitive functioning in natural environments. The initiative will help schools and families identify nearby public lands and waters, and connect with programs that support youth outings. This also will provide K–12 teachers with educational materials, including science labs, lesson plans, and field trip guides.

Ideally, this initiative will evolve beyond fourth grade. In the meantime, government, parent-teacher organizations, conservation groups, and others can increase their efforts to educate the nation's educators, parents, and grandparents about already-existing discount passes for families with kids of all ages.

To locate a park or other natural federal land, go to the Find a Park web page of the National Park Service or to FindYourPark.com.

WILDER STILL

· ·

T he wild is as much a state of mind as a physical place; it can be large or small, "a world in a grain of sand" or "heaven in a wild flower," as William Blake described it; a universe of pines, a fifteen-thousand-foot peak, the plains of Kansas or the Sea of Cortez. These are among the gifts that nature gives each of us, and our children, if we show up.

Step It Up

🍂 **Use nearby urban nature as a gateway to bigger challenges.**
Taking your family on shorter urban nature adventures is a first step for the physical and mental preparation necessary for longer and more strenuous outdoor adventures. Dan Koeppel helped start an urban hiking trend with his famous *Backpacker* magazine article, "I Climbed Los Angeles," which described how he trained for a climb up Mt. Whitney by practicing on several outdoor staircases. "All these steps," he thought, "could add up to a mountain."

🍂 **Go long-distance trekking.**
In Europe, extended hikes of groups or individuals are sometimes called walking tours, which originated in the Romantic movement of the late eighteenth and early nineteenth centuries.

Long-distance hikes are also called trekking or tramping. In the United States, long-distance hikes have been popularized by such books as *Wild* and *A Walk in the Woods*, tales of the Pacific Crest Trail and the Appalachian Trail, respectively. Such hikes are possible, though potentially harrowing, for families with children. For more information, consult the American Hiking Society or a good hiking guide, such as John McKinney's *Joy of Hiking*.

🌿 Take a wilderness night hike.

The wilderness night hike takes the family moonwalk a step farther. At IslandWood, the previously mentioned nature education center on Bainbridge Island, Washington, Riley Hopeman leads his students on hikes at night, the darker the better. "Walking along the trails without a light, we travel together in a uniform pack as the natural world forces a bond we rarely experience," he writes. "We are more dependent upon one another than ever before. Each person is focused, each person is present. Throughout the night hike our lack of nighttime adaptations unites us and as we approach the end of our journey the students have changed."

🌿 Join a group or organization that sponsors family nature trips.

Especially for parents with little prior experience outdoors, or families that have recently moved to a new part of the country or world, experiencing wilderness can be intimidating. Joining others for organized experiences can be particularly helpful, especially for more vigorous outings. Check out Sierra Club's family wilderness trips and other outdoor adventures, including hikes, camping trips, vacations, and volunteer options.

Set Up Camp

🌿 Camping novice? No problem.

Join a "first-time camper" program. State, regional, and national parks around the country make it easy to take the first step. For example, Georgia State Parks offers such a program for families or individuals for (as of this writing) $50, which includes two nights' accommodations, expert advice and help setting up camp, and an emergency phone number.

🌿 Make a family camp plan.

As with hiking, younger children will be more invested and enthusiastic if they help plan the trip. Stay positive and organized, and make sure everyone knows exactly how to get back to the tent by pointing out nearby landmarks. Insist supplies get returned to their designated areas. Talk about how to stay safe (kids should carry whistles) and how to deal with any potentially dangerous animals in the area. Assign kids important chores.

🌿 Camping is play.

Frisbees are dirt cheap, weigh next to nothing, are basically indestructible, and provide hours of fun. Squirt guns are appropriate for hot climates. Footballs and soccer balls are good additions. Smartphones and video games? Each family is different. Success has less to do with what parents take away than with the experiences they provide. A later chapter explores how some tech gadgets, including digital cameras, can help all of us make the nature connection. But nothing quite beats telling ghost stories around a campfire.

🌿 Explore nature just outside the tent or van.

Your family doesn't need to go far from camp to learn about the outdoors. Help your young children look for bugs, birds, and other critters. Identify them in your field guides—books or apps. Check to see if there are any park rangers giving evening lectures close to your campground and attend. Park rangers share their love for camping and the outdoors.

Go glamping.

If you're short on camping gear, or have discomfort-averse family members, or just want an easy way to experience nature without all the planning, cooking, setup, teardown, and cleaning, go "glamping" (glamorous camping), a compromise between wilderness experience and luxury. Most glamping happens in permanent or semipermanent structures like yurts, tree houses, or cabins. It can also be controversial. Some critics object when public park sites are set aside for glamping, and are marked off-limits to people who prefer more rustic and less expensive accommodations. Check for outfitters at Glamping.com.

Tents not your thing? Consider a cabin, lodge, or RV camper.

Cabins can range from rough shelters without bathrooms or running water, available at many parks, to the great lodges such as Old Faithful Inn at Yellowstone and El Tovar Lodge, built on the rim of the Grand Canyon in 1905. These might not be your idea of roughing it, but they're adventures in their own right. TravelAndLeisure.com provides an excellent guide to the national parks lodges and offers this tidbit: "The El Tovar staff once had to hush Paul McCartney because a guest complained about his piano playing." Another option is to camp on wheels, in an RV, trailer, or camper van. Volkswagen may no longer make the classic Westfalia or EuroVan camper van, but Camper-Van-Fun.com describes a world of van conversions. For a guide to RV camping sites, see GoodSamClub.com.

Get Wet and Wetter

🌿 **Learn to swim.**

A surprising number of children never learn to swim. The Ocean Discovery Institute in San Diego found that 90 percent of inner-city children did not know how to swim, 95 percent had never been in a boat, and 34 percent had never even been to the ocean, despite the Pacific being only minutes away. Public swimming pools are a great place to start; they're controlled environments, usually with lifeguards on duty, and swimming instruction programs. Lakes, ponds, and the ocean are free alternatives, but watch out for unpredictable depths, jagged rocks, broken glass, and, in the case of the beach, riptides and dangerously high surf. Start slowly, with flotation devices. And remember, despite the risk at the front end, learning to swim is a basic safety requirement for life. For the more adventurous, snorkeling and scuba diving open up new worlds. SwimLessons.com can guide you to swimming schools and instructors. Or visit a community YMCA.

🌿 **Sail away.**

Any activity close to water ignites the natural senses. In terms of connecting to nature, boating can cut both ways. On lakes or seas, motorboats put us in contact with fish, whales, snakes, water-birds, and humbling weather. But a proviso: high-decibel, high-speed boating can also be a barrier between people and nature, and not only for the people on the boat. Sailing is a quieter option. For general information, see SailingWithKids.net. To learn about accessible sailing, see DisabledSportsUSA.org.

🌿 **Go surfing or paddling.**

If you Google "surfing," most of the hits are about surfing the web. Still, reality-based surfing survives and even thrives. Kids can learn early; adults anytime. Take your kids boogie boarding or skim boarding. Go canoeing or kayaking on salt water or freshwater. Or try paddle boarding: imagine a big surfboard that you stand on and propel yourself with a canoe paddle. Some people fish or photograph from paddleboards, and from surfboards, kayaks, and, of course, canoes, too. Suggested books: *Surf's Up: The Girl's Guide to Surfing*; *Surfer's Start-Up*; *Kayaking Made Easy*; and *Basic Canoeing*.

🍃 **Experience rafting on whitewater rivers or quieter waters.**

Whether you purchase your own raft (and safety equipment) or rent, river rafting is guaranteed to be memorable. Start in easy water—slow moving, no rapids, no major obstacles—and work up from there. Bring squirt guns and waterproof nature guides. The website of Colorado Rafting shares tips for taking a child whitewater rafting. Unless you are experienced, go whitewater rafting with a reputable service, not alone. Or, MotherEarthNews.com provides instructions for building a DIY raft, Huck Finn style, preferably for use on a lake, pond, or slow, shallow stream. Suggested books: *Whitewater Rafting: The Essential Guide to Equipment and Techniques* and *Whitewater Safety and Rescue*.

Ride and Roll

🍃 **Try mountain biking.**

Whether you're buying a new or used street bike or a mountain bike, go for quality, and buy helmets—and *not* used ones. They may look fine, but if they've hit the pavement once, you can't rely on their safety. For mountain bikes, large tires are safer. If you're teaching a child, keep in mind that regular biking skills don't necessarily transfer well. Start slowly by riding in a local park or on a level trail. Move up in difficulty gradually until you can start tackling technical challenges. Keep an eye on energy and morale, take breaks often, take water, and stay on the trail: don't damage nature or the nature experience of others. See the website of the International Mountain Biking Association for its rules of the trail. Suggested book: *The Art of Mountain Biking.*

🍃 **Ride a horse.**

Horseback riding is a great way to travel through natural areas. You're more likely to use all your senses, and bonding with a horse is more interesting than bonding with a car, even a Prius. Horseback riding is often used as a form of therapy for people with special needs. Learn more about equine-assisted activities and therapies from the Professional Association of Therapeutic Horsemanship International (PATH Intl.), the American Hippotherapy Association, and the Federation of Horses in Education and Therapy International.

Extreme Outdoor Sports in the Millennial Age

....

Here's the conventional wisdom. Once children turn into teenagers, they lose interest in nature and focus on a different kind of biology more often found at the mall. But teenagers can also build on the nature experiences they've had as children. Young people are more likely to be attracted to riskier outdoor adventures, such as snorkeling, kayaking, surfing, windsurfing, waterskiing, wakeboarding, scuba diving, and river rafting.

Outdoor industry research suggests that nature-engaged millennials often view nature as a theme park for advanced snowboarding or high-intensity rock climbing, and prefer that to more-traditional outdoor sports, such as fishing, hunting, or birding.

Do extreme outdoor sports really connect young people to nature? It depends. Some young people (and adults) plug their ears with earbuds when participating in outdoor sports, obscuring part of the experience.

But others report a different kind of communion: immersion in nature with the added attraction of risk. While discovering the physical, psychological benefits of green exercise, some become *more* aware of their surroundings. Extreme outdoor sports may even be going through a transition experienced by surfers a few decades ago, toward a deeper, perhaps even spiritual experience in nature.

Glenn D. Hoagland, executive director of New York's Mohonk Preserve, reports that young rock climbers and mountain bikers have surprised him. "I've realized how in touch rock climbers are with the rock itself. They become very aware of and protective of rare cliff-face plants, like mountain spleenwort, and [of] nesting birds, like peregrine falcons—and even the five-lined skink." He also says that some young mountain bikers practice "slow and quiet" biking and adopt stringent rules of personal conduct, safety, and stewardship.

Go to Extremes

🍃 **Go skiing, cross-country skiing, snowboarding, or mountainboarding.**
Some ski runs let young kids ski for free, and most offer lessons. Taking multiday lessons or joining a ski club (many offer group discounts) can introduce a young person (or other novice) to the sport. A mountainboard or dirtboard is basically a revved-up skateboard with bigger wheels. You race down hillsides rather than on streets. Like skiers and snowboarders, mountainboarders generally go too fast to stop and smell the wildflowers, but wind and speed and falling down are part of nature, too. *Ski Magazine* offers an online family guide to skiing at Skinet.com.

🍃 **Go rock and mountain climbing.**
Learn about ropes, anchors, and belays; no-rope climbing; and more. Recommended book: *How to Rock Climb!*, which is part of a

series of books on climbing. If you and your kids enjoy rock climbing, you might love mountain climbing. Indoor climbing gyms are good places to start. After you're familiar with the use of climbing equipment and your strength and endurance have improved, take it outdoors and try climbing a boulder. Increase the difficulty of climbs incrementally. Invest in good harnesses, helmets, and shoes, and don't push children too hard. MEC, a Canadian outdoor gear supplier and co-op founded by mountaineers, offers an online "Climbing with Kids" guide.

Extreme tree climbing and ziplining.
Solitary tree climbing can be a spiritual experience, exhilarating, and harrowing. (Read John Muir's account of spending hours in a tree during a major windstorm.) But for the most challenging tree climbing, take lessons. One example: Cornell's Youth Recreational Tree Climbing course, for kids ages eight to eighteen, teaches the basics of using ropes and rappelling in trees. Some tree-climbing trainers offer group rates to Scouts and other youth organizations, and family nature clubs. Tree Climbers International helps people of all ages make friends in high places, often using sophisticated climbing gear to reach the highest branches hundreds of feet above the ground. According to TCI, "There are many reasons why people climb trees. For some, it's a way to relax and get away from it all, or to do some enhanced birding. For others, tree climbing is a career choice, such as tree work or canopy research." WorldwideZipline.com publishes an online guide to ziplining companies. Keep in mind that the zipline industry is mostly unregulated by government, though most U.S. companies follow industry standards, according to NBC.

Hang tough.
Hang gliding and paragliding are thrilling activities for older kids and their braver parents. Along with safety information, the U.S. Hang Gliding and Paragliding Association publishes a list of gliding schools at ushpa.org. For the extra daring, skydiving and

bungee jumping are now well-established sports, and accidents are rare. For the extra-extra daring, take a look at wingsuit flying (where you look like a flying squirrel). "I was always intrigued by birds as a kid, and now I know how it feels to fly," says Brook Hopper, a thirty-one-year-old leader in the outdoor sports industry who started wingsuit flying in her early twenties. "I become a bird. I see the world as a bird does, and it is in this time that I am truly present and fully aware." For everyone else, hot air ballooning is another way to see the world below.

🍃 **Activate extreme abilities.**

As with most of the activities recommended in this book, extreme outdoor sports—from skiing to rock climbing to hang gliding—can be adapted for people with disabilities. As described on DisabledSportsUSA.org, adaptive climbing is a popular sport among amputees who use prostheses or go without. Brent Kuemmerle, an experienced adaptive climber, was a climber before he was injured in a car accident that resulted in a leg amputation. "Climbing motivated me to get out of the hospital and resume what I was doing," he says. "I'm at a higher level of climbing today than I was when I had two legs." Recommended book: *Climbing Back*.

NURTURE YOUR INNER HUNTER & GATHERER

Biologically, we're still hunters and gatherers. So how do we feed that gene? Hunting and fishing are the traditional ways. Many families bond through these outdoor activities. In fact, fishing is still the number one gateway activity that connects kids to nature. However, these sports aren't everyone's cup of chamomile tea, so alternatives are offered below. Consider these hunting and gathering activities that help in the development of strong children and adults, possibly enhancing the senses.

Go hunting, the old-fashioned way.

While many people disapprove, hunting is gaining advocates from some former critics, who make this argument: If you're going to eat meat, it's better to hunt for or raise your own than to depend on factory farms. And controlled hunting in urban places is increasingly seen as a necessary activity to protect biodiversity, as feral pigs and deer overpopulate and push out threatened wild species. If you decide to introduce hunting to your kids, or if you're already a hunter, emphasize gun safety and the ethical standards of hunting. Resources on hunting ethics include *Field & Stream* magazine's website, where you can read How to Teach Your Child Hunting Ethics. South Carolina's Department of Natural Resources provides a good list of rules of conduct.

Go fish.

In his outdoor blog for EurekaTent.com, my son Matt Louv captures the magic (and the ulterior motive) of angling with this line: "Birds, plants and clouds all go well with fish." For kids five and younger, expect and encourage them to occasionally put the rod down and poke along the water's edge. For older kids, start with the simplest techniques and gear. Bend down the barbs on the hooks for safety—this also makes it easier to release fish unharmed if you prefer. Many anglers practice catch-and-release (some fly-fishers even use flies with no hooks, to simply feel the thrill of the strike) whereas others believe that the only ethical reason to fish is for the food you'll eat that day. A related activity is crawdadding. Tie a piece of liver or bacon to a string, drop it into a creek or pond, and wait until you feel a tug. No hooks needed. From the crawdad's point of view, pinch-and-release is preferred. A good resource is TakeMeFishing.org. For learning about catch-and-release and other approaches to fishing, see the Angling Unlimited website. Recommended Book: *Gone Fishin' with Kids: How to Take Your Kid Fishing and Still Be Friends.*

🍃 Practice Deep Fishing

Some anglers pursue what might be called "deep fishing," which employs more of the senses, a quieter approach, fewer engines, and more focus on a wider range of human senses. Women and their daughters make up the fastest-growing group in fly-fishing, and guides often prefer them as clients because some are more willing to learn than some men, and they tend to approach the water differently—taking time to study the water, weather, insects and other wildlife that offer clues to fishing conditions. The "deep fishing" approach can be applied to any outdoor sport or activity.

🍃 Go bishing, phishing, or knishing.

If one family member fishes, and another doesn't, go bishing (one birds while the other fishes) or phishing (one fishes; the other does wildlife photography), or knishing (one fishes; the other knits). My wife and I do all three.

Snakeability

••••••••••••••••••••••••••

S ome older kids and adults (even people with a snake phobia, which gives this activity a certain . . . edge) love to snake hunt. That doesn't mean killing snakes. It does mean finding them in their natural habitat—and observing them or catching, studying, and releasing them. If you are not absolutely certain of the species, enjoy observing from a safe distance.

Use a snake stick (a hoe will do) to turn over flat rocks and logs, or snake tongs to handle the snake. Wear high boots or snake chaps, and carry a gunnysack for collecting. The best policy, though, is to leave the snake where it is, take a few photographs, and replace the log or rock as you found it. Venomous snakebite fatalities are relatively rare, but always be cautious.

Harry W. Greene, professor of ecology and evolutionary biology at Cornell University, and author of seminal books on snakes, advises, "Generally once you've seen a venomous snake and as long as you don't pick it up or otherwise harass the animal, it's no longer of any danger—just step back and appreciate your good fortune to have encountered one of nature's most amazing creatures."

More safety tips: Be sure you can see where your feet and hands are going. Don't step blindly over logs or rocks, or reach into crevices. Avoid walking through tall grass unless you're wearing adequate protection. If you are bitten, don't try to suck out the venom or cut the wound (as falsely portrayed in movies); don't drink alcohol or take blood-thinning medications. If bitten on a hand, remove rings, bracelets, and watches without delay, as swelling can sometimes occur quickly. Call for help on your cell phone or radio, and seek medical attention immediately.

AllTrails.com offers an online guide for finding snakes. For a snakebite fact sheet, see AmericanHiking.org. Suggested books: *Snakes: The Evolution of Mystery in Nature*; Smithsonian's *Everything You Need to Know About Snakes and Other Scaly Reptiles*; *Snakes! A Kid's Book of Cool Images and Amazing Facts About Snakes*; and *A Field Guide to Western Reptiles and Amphibians*.

BE A WILDWATCHER

There's more than one way to unleash your or your child's inner hunter and gatherer. As a hobby, wildwatching stimulates the senses, teaches you how to move quietly in the woods or fields, and connects you more intimately to where you live. Some people combine wildwatching with drawing, journaling, or photography. Observe raccoons in the backyard (don't feed them), coyotes in urban areas, whales and seabirds at sea. Learning to track, follow sign, and stalk wildlife is, according to Princeton University's Outdoor Action program, a sacred responsibility: "Getting too close to animals can cause serious disturbances including: abandoning young, disturbing nesting grounds, damaging foraging areas."

🌿 **Pursue the art of tracking and following animal sign.**

Tracking and understanding the signs that wild animals leave behind can be done by all ages and at multiple skill levels. Learn to read the tracks of the largest predators or the smallest birds. Observe and see if an acorn has been split by a human foot or a deer hoof, or if it has been gnawed by a specific species of squirrel. Some camps and wilderness-training schools teach sophisticated techniques for tracking and reading sign. Among the better-known schools for learning about tracking and following sign: the Ndakinna Education Center, A Naturalist's World, and the Wilderness Awareness School.

Suggested books and resources: Wildlifetrackers.com; *Mammal Tracks & Sign: A Guide to North American Species*; *Tracking and the Art of Seeing*; and for kids, *Big Tracks, Little Tracks*, and *Keepers of the Animals: Native American Stories and Wildlife Activities for Children*.

🌿 **Be a still-hunter.**

Still-hunting is the practice of sitting still in nature and waiting for animals to appear. You can do it in your backyard sit spot, or in the wilderness. As a wildwatcher, the purpose is simply to watch or take photographs. Still-hunters are unobtrusive and try to make themselves part of nature. This practice takes patience and can be extremely rewarding. In the right setting—beside a river during a salmon run, for example, or beside a shallow creek or pond—fishing-watching is possible, too. If you and your kids return to the same still-hunting spot multiple times, keep a journal of your observations. You can also set up a blind—a tent or small structure with peepholes. Or you can work with a conservation group to create something more elaborate, what the British call a wildlife watching "hide," which typically holds several people (often serious photography enthusiasts). They can be made as huts, large tents, or mobile structures that can be pulled by car, horse, or four-wheel drive vehicle. Some are built on runners or skis. RewildingEurope.com offers an online guide to building more sophisticated hides.

🌿 Be a birder.

Traditionally a hobby for mature adults, birding can also be a great activity for you and your children. In contrast to some other outdoor activities, birding may be gaining ground with young people. Part of this growth is due to the advent of compact field guides and digital cameras, as well as electronic applications that help simplify species identification in the field. But specialized gear is not required. For a list of birding clubs in North America, visit the American Birding Association website. For international birding and ornithological organizations, visit Wildbirds.com.

🌿 Learn to talk with the animals.

Naturalist and teacher Jon Young describes a hidden world of bird communication rich with nuance and decipherable information. He advises: Take your child to his or her sit spot in nature or encourage your child to go there alone. To talk with the birds, Young recommends sitting for thirty to forty minutes a day, three days a week or more. At first, the birds make only a few sounds. "Sit as still as possible. You won't have to wait long to start noticing movement and sound," he advises. When the birds have fully acclimated, the visiting human will experience what's called the birds' "baseline," the suite of behaviors and vocalizations that birds express when they perceive no threats from their environment. Young discerns five different categories of bird vocalization: songs, companion calls, territorial aggression, adolescent begging, and alarms. With practice, family members will be able to track the movements of unseen bird predators based on alarm calls alone. To learn more, read Young's book, *What the Robin Knows.*

Set an insect trap.

As with all animal collecting, the best policy is to catch, study, and release insects. The simplest way to trap them is to put a large white sheet under a tree and shake the branches. Along with the leaf litter that falls on the sheet, look for a diverse bunch of microbeasts. Or use a sheet, clothesline, and light source to attract insects at night with a light trap, or, with a jar and household items, create a bug vacuum or pitfall to capture and study insects without hurting them. Your kids can also keep an eye out for the insects that do their own trapping, like trapdoor spiders or ant lions. To find ant lions, look for loose dirt or fine-grain sand in areas without much foot traffic, and you may find their small, conical pits. To learn how to collect and study insects, check out the Wildlife Watch website for plans for insect traps and other DIY wildwatching gear. Recommended books: *Kaufman Field Guide to Insects of North America* and *The Insect Book: A Basic Guide to the Collection and Care of Common Insects for Young Children.*

Collect fireflies at dusk; release them later that night.

Fireflies, a.k.a. lightning bugs, are actually beetles, and there are two thousand species of fireflies around the world. In some species, the eggs and larvae glow, too. At night, your kids can catch fireflies using a butterfly net. Place them in a jar with a lid pierced to let in air and a moist napkin or paper towel for humidity. Today, firefly numbers are dwindling, according to Firefly.org, which offers instructions on safe ways to catch and release. Recommended book: *Living Lights: Fireflies in Your Backyard.*

Spot reptiles, amphibians, and other wildlife on a nighttime nature drive.

In the spring or fall, especially after a rain or when the road warms and holds the daytime heat, drive slowly at night on a deserted road and watch carefully in the path of your car's headlights. Depending on the geography and the season, you and your kids may be able to identify snakes, geckos, toads, salamanders, kangaroo rats, and other nocturnal animals attracted to the heat of the road. If you get out of your car, watch for venomous snakes and other cars. A related activity: save the tortoises and turtles. In some areas of the country, endangered box turtles migrate in the spring. Countless tortoises (and other critters) are killed by cars. Especially after a spring rain, drive the back roads and move them out of harm's way. Suggested link: the North American Amphibian Monitoring Program.

Trap footprints.

Fill a baking sheet with moist sand and leave a dish of cat or dog food in the center. Then, leave it outside for the night and return with your children the next day to see if anybody was hungry. Or take three juice or milk cartons, cut off the tops and bottoms, and fit them together to make a tunnel. Line the bottom of the tunnel with white paper, and cut a sponge to fit into a margarine tub lid. Soak the sponge in colored dye, place a small amount of food on the sponge, and put the sponge inside the tunnel. Camouflage the whole thing with foliage and leave it outside overnight, somewhere where you suspect critters may traffic. In the morning, check to see who was caught red-pawed (or purple, or green). Because it's not a good idea to feed wild animals, trapping footprints should not be done on a regular basis. Wildlife Watch, in the UK, provides instructions. Takeachildoutside.org tells how to make a plaster cast of a track.

Go hiking with Bigfoot, if you can find him—or her.

Whether you're a Bigfoot believer or not, trying to rub elbows with one will take you to some of the most beautiful places in the world. This is one way to pique a kid's interest in the outdoors. Here are some suggestions from my son Matt, an occasional guide in Alaska: Check the Bigfoot Field Researchers Organization's sighting map to find eyewitness accounts close to where you live or where you plan to travel. Pick an area with reported activity, and hike, back-pack, or camp there at a place and time of year when berries are ripe, where ferns, water plants, and other edibles are plentiful. Try hitting the trunk of a tree with a large piece of wood and quietly wait a few minutes to see if anything knocks back. Keep your ears open for whoops and screams, your nose open for unfamiliar, pungent odors. And if, by some chance, you do run into Bigfoot, don't provoke him — or her. No Sasquatch jokes.

PRACTICE WILDCRAFTING

A term that originally meant gaining skill and knowledge in wilderness survival, "wildcrafting" has come to be used more specifically as the hunting and gathering of plants in their wild state, for food, herbal medicines, or crafts. This isn't your grandmother's leaf collecting and pressing (that's fun, too) but a more sophisticated interaction with nature, requiring patience, careful observation, and a cultivated knowledge of species identification.

🍃 Forage for herbs and other plants in the city.
Lest you think wildcrafting is strictly a rural phenomenon, there's a strong urban foraging movement. Urban foragers are inspired by motivations such as "maintaining cultural practices, sharing knowledge, building community, engaging in spiritual practices, and connecting with nature," says researcher Melissa R. Poe and colleagues writing in the journal *Human Ecology*. To learn more about urban foragers, visit BiophilicCities.com or FallingFruit. org, which describes itself as a "massive, collaborative map of the urban harvest." Supported by a growing user community, it offers an online map pointing to more than half a million food sources around the world "from plants and fungi to water wells and Dumpsters."

Go mushroom hunting.

Mushrooms "fruit" year-round, and come in all sorts of bizarre shapes and colors. Depending on the area, the best time to hunt for mushrooms is after a heavy rain in the fall or early winter. Take photos, or collect a few mushrooms to make "spore prints" — cut the cap from the stem of any medium or large mushroom and set the cap gills-down over a sheet of paper. Cover the cap with a glass or bowl and let it sit overnight. The mushroom will deposit a layer of spores that will make a beautiful sunburst pattern on the paper. Toxic mushrooms can be extremely difficult to differentiate from nontoxic ones, so if your family is inclined to eat wild mushrooms, only collect mushrooms with an expert mushroom hunter. Mother Earth News offers an online guide to mushrooms. Suggested book: *The Complete Mushroom Hunter.*

Be an ethical gatherer.

Ethical, safety-conscious wildcrafting connects children to nature directly. They see where food comes from and learn the basics of sustainability. John Lust, in *The Natural Remedy Bible*, advises that wildcrafters "harvest where the plant appears to be thriving, as that is where we will be able to find the strongest plants," and to "be sure to leave enough so that the plant can easily recover its growth."

Whatever form of hunting and gathering your family chooses, the main thing is to capture memories for the future.

On the River: The Restorative Power of Nature in Difficult Times

....

On the banks of California's Owens River, my younger son, Matthew, then twenty-three, and I were trying to cure our nature-deficit disorder. That day, we staggered across the clumped grass and mud along the river and struggled to keep our balance as 40 mph gusts tangled our fly lines. We froze and sweated in the sleet as the snow line crept lower on the Sierra. Fishing was terrible, we were miserably cold, and perfectly happy.

As we fished, I thought about an earlier time for us on this river.

When the Twin Towers fell, Matthew was thirteen. That afternoon, I bundled him into the VW van and took him to this very place. His brother was off at college by then, otherwise I would have done the same with him. We fled from the great pain that would lead to greater pain, and drove the six hours from San Diego to the Owens, and parked next to the current that washed out all the sound and all the fury. That night, inside the van, we flipped down the table and ate granola bars and drank hot chocolate and watched the window screens grow opaque with a late hatch of insects.

And all the next day and the day after that, we cut the electrical cord to the outside world, and found a sense of equilibrium.

Sven Lindblad, who heads Lindblad Expeditions, which works in partnership with National Geographic, once told me that, even as other cruise ship companies took a dive following 9/11, his ships, which focus exclusively on the wonders of nature—of the Galápagos, the Antarctic, and other points of interest—filled up with clients. In the days following the trauma, families with children were especially drawn to the natural world, and he credits them with saving his business.

Not everyone has the ability to seek out nature in difficult times. One must acknowledge that inequity, and another reality: the people who lost their homes to Hurricane Sandy or the people of the drowned parishes of New Orleans or the irradiated mud fields of post-tsunami Japan found no solace in the natural world.

Still, in dark times, one human impulse is to find kinship with other species and connection to elements beyond the headlines, where we feel larger forces at work, and know that all things must pass.

At the saturation point, the rush of water on a stream, a sudden storm on a high trail, or a discovered quiet corner of an urban park is preferable to the inundation of media coverage that, hour after hour, repeats itself, until our response to the pain on the screen seems to move beyond empathetic to gratuitous. How much of modern life is spent adrift in vicarious experience, secondhand reality, the pain of endless war brought to you by liquid cleansers?

We do need to know about world events and tragedies manmade and natural, and there is no ignorance quite so unattractive as prideful ignorance.

But we also need respite from the kind of media static that so often seems drained of reality. In a virtual world where information overload is more accurately described as information underload, a little raw authenticity and gratitude can be a welcome relief.

So perhaps we can be excused for escaping the bad news for a few hours or days, as we lean into the wind slashing across the river, or see a trout rise, or watch a Harrier hawk glide close along a field, and on the long walk home step over the perfectly white bones of a cow that has not survived the winter, though we have, and not only survived but thrived.

Other Voices

"My wife and I were hiking on Mt. Washburn in Yellowstone National Park and met a group of multi-racial teenagers who were part of the Overland Summer Program. They were from cities all over the U.S. and, with the Overland leaders, were filled with an excitement and energy that I rarely see in teens in their daily lives in school. It was the first wilderness experience for each of them . . . The focus is on using the wilderness experience to help at-risk kids. But the fact is that most of our teens are in some way at risk and can benefit equally from these programs."

— Mark Phillips, retired professor of education,
San Francisco State University, columnist, Edutopia

"Like any four-year-old, Amelie gets tired and likes to ride in my backpack on many of our outdoor adventures. For our wilderness trip, we discussed how this would be a great opportunity for her to climb unassisted. She vowed that she would make it on her own.

We decided to tackle Dorothy Lake, which is about a 1,200-foot climb. When we got to the trailhead, Amelie put on her small backpack and trotted out onto the trail with her loyal scout, our dog, Mocha. She soon came to a wilderness sign and asked, 'If this is wilderness, why is there a sign, Daddy?' When I explained that it was to let people know they are in wilderness, she replied, 'Well, as long as it does not hurt the tree, we are OK. We need the trees to breathe.'"

— Martin LeBlanc, Seattle, Washington

Part 6

. . . .

Grow Outside:
The Nature Prescription

"We need the tonic of wildness."

— HENRY DAVID THOREAU

"If nature contact were a medication, we would be prescribing it to everybody."

— HOWARD FRUMKIN,
DEAN OF THE SCHOOL OF PUBLIC HEALTH
AT THE UNIVERSITY OF WASHINGTON

HEALTHY BY NATURE

· ·

Time spent in nature isn't a panacea for everything that ails us, but it does offer some special properties. In 2013, in a presentation at an event focused on children and nature, G. Richard Olds, MD, dean of the University of California, Riverside, Medical School, made this point: Few medications or prescriptions work *both* as prevention and as therapy.

The most fundamental health benefit of spending time with nature is that it gets us off the couch and moving. Diet and genetics contribute to obesity, but so does simple inactivity—and prolonged sitting may be a killer even if we don't put on the pounds. In July 2012, the *Lancet,* a prestigious British medical journal, launched a series of alarming reports, confirming that physical inactivity is a leading risk factor for deaths due to non-communicable diseases. The journal reported that the pandemic of inactivity is causing 5.3 million deaths per year, comparable to the number of deaths attributed to tobacco smoking—and that the risk of inactivity to health is similar to the risk posed by tobacco use. Add to this list of maladies the harm to psychological health and cognitive skills, which in turn can exacerbate health problems and contribute to weight gain.

In other words, sitting is the new smoking.

As a result of this unsettling news, standing desks, including those attached to treadmills, have become popular, at least, popular in the media. They may be a passing fad. And though they're the antithesis of sitting, they're only part of the solution to the pandemic of inactivity. For a more cost-effective, full body, mind, and soul treatment, get some green exercise. It's a lot more fun.

Pediatricians, in particular, are moving quickly on this front.

Stephen Pont, MD, chair of the American Academy of Pediatrics Section on Obesity, is particularly concerned about what he and other health officials now call the pandemic of inactivity: "Connecting with nature has been an important part of my life and I encourage my patients to do the same," he says." The more nature experiences they have, the more healthy habits they adopt."

Nature Play Prescription

Dr._____

Name:_____ Date:_____

Your Healthcare Provider encourages you to:

· Go outside and play in nature.
· Limit your "Screen Time" to no
  more than 60 minutes each day.
· Read stories about nature.
  (Or have someone read them to you)

Signed:_____
Provider:_____
Parent/Child:_____

In Holland, Michigan, Paul Dykema, MD, changed his pediatrics clinic waiting area to include posters about reconnecting children and nature, for their health and well-being. He provides a waiting room video about the benefits to children and families from nature-based experiences; incorporates recommendations for nature-based time outdoors in all the regular family wellness meetings for parents and children from birth and older; and has a special instruction pad for children, prescribing an hour a day of outdoor play in nature, and twenty minutes of reading a day.

What can we do? We can partner with physicians and other health professionals to promote the health benefits of getting outdoors for our own families and communities, and we can start in and around our own homes.

CREATE YOUR OWN NATURE GYM

Most of us recognize that exercising is a cost-effective way to improve the health of children and adults. But exercising outside in nature offers added benefits, not only for children but also for the rest of us as we age. Comparison between people exercising on indoor treadmills and people burning the same number of calories doing green exercise showed that those exercising outdoors made even better improvements in their health. Explanations for these benefits, and many others, vary—from theories involving brain function and genetic programming, to everyday common sense.

🌿 **Garden for fitness.**
For people of all ages, the health benefits of gardening are well established. Some studies of aging suggest that people who spend time in the garden are offered some protection from Alzheimer's disease. If your family doesn't have a garden, offer to pull weeds in a friend's or neighbor's garden—and take the kids with you. Or volunteer at a local botanical garden or at one of the community gardens. Some of the most popular community gardens were born

in some of the most densely populated and economically stressed neighborhoods. These gardens are important sources of nutrition, physical and psychological health, and friendship-building. Community gardens also serve as nature gyms, especially if natural exercise features are added.

🍃 Take it outside with friends and family.

Groups of friends and families (and family nature clubs) can organize for regular green exercise, using the Internet or the old-fashioned telephone to choose where to meet—a hiking or walking trail, someone's backyard garden, a stream reclamation project, a kayaking trip. Studies show that experiencing nature together can build social ties and a sense of community and place. As individuals, or as a family or other group, volunteer with a local park to help maintain a walking or hiking trail. That's the kind of exercise that builds something larger than muscles.

🍃 Create a nature gym in the backyard or other green area.

Natural elements can provide visually and physically attractive ways to exercise that can augment or replace that weight machine filling up half the garage. Rocks to lift. Strong trees for arm-presses and pull-ups. Logs for stepping exercises, or to support you during pushups, or to increase core strength through balance. Hillsides for "hill squats," as the author of *Tina Vindum's Outdoor Fitness* calls them. In a densely urban neighborhood, strong green roofs and rooftop gardens can serve triple purposes: garden, play space, and nature gym.

🍃 Hire a green exercise trainer.

Some personal trainers specialize in outdoor workouts. If you don't like gyms but aren't sure how to exercise outdoors effectively, finding a green exercise guide will be worth the investment. And if you want to save some money, try a group outdoor exercise class.

🍃 Join an organized Green Gym program.

An organization called BTCV Green Gyms sponsors environmental conservation volunteering throughout the UK and around the world. Participants boost their physical strength and stamina as they tackle useful outdoor conservation and nature restoration projects under the guidance of experienced leaders. The idea is spreading. Conservation Volunteers Australia encourages nature as an alternative to traditional gym programs and organized sports. Adam Smolak, a project officer of Conservation Volunteers Australia, told *Women's Health & Fitness* magazine, "If you want to dig up five garden beds, you can go as hard as you like and you'll be worn out . . . We've weeded in the gardens for two hours followed by a two km walk."

🍃 Go natural, or just move the machines outdoors.

Some municipalities, particularly in China and the UK, have set up traditional exercise machines in parks and other public places, sometimes near children's playgrounds, which, as the *Guardian* reports, "encourages parents to use them while the kids play." Other parks offer chin-up bars and sit-up planks. Natural objects, such as anchored logs, can also be used for exercise. Running trails are less intrusive.

🍃 Develop a sense of balance, off road.

Kelli Calabrese, a Texas-based trainer and coauthor of the book *Feminine, Firm & Fit,* explains why outdoor terrain trumps indoor machines. "Machines are created to make it easier on you, but the ground forces you to adjust to whatever the elements have done to it," she says. "Literally every section of a hill is different and will work your calves a little differently." Pilates, yoga, and tai chi can also be practiced outdoors. Suggested books: *The Outdoor Athlete* and *Pilates for the Outdoor Athlete.*

Is There a Recommended Dose of Vitamin N?

••••••••••••••••••••••••••••••••••

P arents often ask that question. So do teachers. Pediatricians, not so much. They know that it's hard enough to count out pills, let alone prescribe a correct number of trees. Still, some researchers are trying to come up with useful recommendations, particularly for stress reduction.

In *The Dirt*, a publication of the American Society of Landscape Architects, Jared Green reported in June 2015 that landscape architects and psychologists are "trying to determine how to prescribe a 'nature pill' . . . for maximum mental and physical health benefits." How long, how frequently, and "what form of nature works best?" A team led by MaryCarol Hunter, a landscape architect and ecologist at the University of Michigan, followed a small sample of forty-four people over eight weeks, asking them to use a custom-designed smartphone app to answer questions about weather, landscapes, what views they preferred, and to take photographs. The app used GPS to track their routes.

The early results of the study "show that the 'nature pill' works," wrote Green. All participants reported significantly less stress, increased ability to focus, better mood and energy levels after being exposed to nature. "But Hunter admitted that 'self-reported data is viewed as worthless; people want physical proof.'" The team also recorded the levels of stress-related cortisol, and these matched the experiences self-reported by the participants more than 60 percent of the time. Weather, by the way, seemed to have no correlation with the restorative effects of time spent in more natural environments.

"Hunter said it's still too soon to tell what the optimal dose of the nature pill is, but even just 'ten minutes is effective,'" added Green.

In 2010, researchers at the UK's University of Essex put that number at five minutes. The results from this more extensive survey by Jo Barton and Jules Pretty was published in the journal *Environmental Science and*

Technology. An analysis of ten studies involving 1,252 people of different ages, gender and mental health status showed green exercise—walking, gardening, cycling, fishing, boating, horse-riding and farming—led to mental and physical health improvements, especially in the young and the mentally ill, though all age and social groups benefited. "For the first time in the scientific literature, we have been able to show dose-response relationships for the positive effects of nature on human mental health," said Pretty. He and Barton recommended green exercise for therapy, improved access to green space, and more educational opportunities for children in outdoor settings. They concluded that Britain's National Health Services should include a "natural health service." Barton put it this way: "A walk a day should help to keep the doctor away—and help to save the country money."

More research is needed. Pinning the dose to five or ten minutes is unlikely to meet the needs of everyone. A more accurate estimate of the correct dose of Vitamin N is: Some is better than none, and more is better than some.

General Outdoor Strategies for Physical and Mental Health

🌿 **Stressed out? Use nature to reduce the impact of toxic stress on children and adults.**

Nature is an antidote to stress—children, parents, just about everyone feels better after spending time in the natural world, even if it's in a backyard or neighborhood park. Researchers in Sweden have found that joggers who exercise in natural green settings, as compared to more manmade environments, feel more restored and less anxious, angry, or depressed. These findings apply in rural, suburban, or urban settings with parks or other open space.

🌿 Consider nature as an added strategy to reduce ADHD symptoms.

Parents, pediatricians, and educators can help children with attention difficulties do better in school and life. Researchers at the University of Illinois suggest nature time as an added or alternative therapy for some children diagnosed with ADHD and other similar conditions.

🌿 If a family member is ill, make sure he or she has a view of nature.

Pennsylvania researchers have found that patients in rooms with tree views had shorter hospitalizations, less need for pain medications, and fewer negative comments in the nurses' notes, compared to patients with views of brick. In most urban settings, window boxes, and even photographs or videos of nature can help.

🌿 Seek out positive places with negative ions.

The reason we feel good at the beach isn't just because of the view. Natural settings such as beaches, waterfalls, even the zoo — if it's rich with plant life and water features — are usually filled with negative ions, invisible and odorless molecules that we inhale. When they reach our bloodstream, negative ions are believed to increase levels of serotonin, which alleviate depression. (On the other hand, some weather conditions such as California's dry Santa Ana winds and Italy's sirocco increase positives ions, which are linked to increases in depression and irritability.)

🌿 Create a therapeutic landscape.

If your family doesn't already have access to a healing natural place, help create one at home, your kids' school, your neighborhood, your workplace, or elsewhere. In 1999, Clare Cooper Marcus and Marni Barnes edited a seminal book called *Healing Gardens*. It pioneered ideas about how to create the now relatively common hospital healing gardens for patients and their families. Marcus, Naomi A. Sachs, and others have continued that work, expanding the concept of therapeutic landscapes to gardens for veterans, restorative planting for public spaces, mental health and behavioral facilities, nursing homes and assisted living facilities, as well as children's hospitals. Horticultural therapy is something that every health-care official, developer, and business and municipal policymaker should consider. Learn more from the Therapeutic Landscapes Network. Suggested book: *Therapeutic Landscapes: An Evidence-Based Approach to Designing Healing Gardens and Restorative Outdoor Spaces.*

Support your local health-care providers who promote nature time.

Parents depend on pediatricians, but pediatricians depend on parents. So support the pediatricians and other health-care professionals, including nurse practitioners, psychologists, occupational therapists, and others who are incorporating nature into their practices. Share information about the health benefits of the nature connection with them, including the list of suggested actions for health-care providers in this book.

Nature Programs
That Offer Peace
and Healing to Veterans
and Their Families

··

S ome of the most inspiring programs that connect people to nature focus on the health of military families. "Getting outside makes coming
home from war easier for our military service members, veterans, and
their families," according to Stacy Bare, director of the Sierra Club's Mission
Outdoors, an effort to connect all Americans to the great outdoors. He served
in Iraq from 2006–07, and received a Bronze Star for merit.

"We know from repeated testimony that increased confidence, family
and social connections, learning how to live with a new physical adaptation,
improved mental health, and even recovery from addiction, are attributed to
time spent in the outdoors by veterans and military families," he writes in
an essay for the Children & Nature Network. "Programs available to military
families include the National Military Family Association's Operation Purple,
and Retreats, Outward Bound for Veterans, the Wounded Warrior Project's
Project Odyssey, and the collaborative effort, 4-H Military Partnerships, a
collaboration between 4-H offices and active duty and reserve.

"Some programs, like Higher Ground and Project Sanctuary, include a
deliberate therapeutic component," writes Bare. "Others, like Project Healing
Waters and Veterans Expeditions, argue that time in the outdoors, fly-fishing
or climbing respectively, inherently provide the therapy. Most programs fall
somewhere in between."

VISIT A NATURE THERAPY RETREAT

A kin to nature gyms, outdoor healing and treatment programs represent an old idea with new cachet. Some are expensive, but the principles can be applied to our homes, schools, workplaces, and neighborhoods. In the UK, former supermodel Sille Lundquist, whose company Being Human runs nature retreats for stressed-out city dwellers, told London's *Daily Mail*: "Five years ago, most of our enquiries were about weight loss. Now when people tick the box on the form about why they're attending, most say they want to de-stress and get back to nature." As with any health service or residential treatment program, assure that they are licensed and inspected regularly by state or provincial health departments.

🌿 **Practice Shinrin-Yoku, or "Forest Bathing."**
In Japan, forest bathing—known as shinrin-yoku—is popular. It's based on the idea that if a person visits a natural area and simply walks in a relaxed way, they will achieve calming, rejuvenating, and restorative benefits. In 1982, the Forest Agency of the Japanese government came up with a shinrin-yoku plan to encourage the populace to get out into nature for mental and physical exercise and stress reduction. In 2006, an organization began to give forests across the country the official designations of Forest Therapy Base or Forest Therapy Road. Visitors can take part in guided walks with experts in forest medicine, or enroll in classes such as dietary management and hydrotherapy, and receive medical checkups. Some Japanese companies send employees to forest therapy bases—presumably to increase their productivity. The therapy forests also attract tourists, which boosts local economies. To find out more about forest bathing and whether it's for you, go to the Healthy Parks Healthy People Central website. Recommended book: *Your Brain on Nature*.

🍃 **Spend time at a nature health farm or retreat.**
"Woodland therapy" and "care farming," partnerships among farmers, health-care providers, and health-care consumers, are taking root in several European countries to care for people and land.

For example, in the UK, a growing "green care" movement encourages therapeutic horticulture, ecotherapy, green-exercise activities, animal-assisted therapies, and green-care farming, which is simply defined as using farms or other agricultural settings to foster better physical and mental health. See the website GreenExercise.org for more information. The UK's National Care Farming Institute offers a directory of therapy farms.

In Norway, general practitioners can prescribe a stay at a care farm for their patients. In the Netherlands, six hundred health farms are integrated into the health service.

The idea is catching on in the United States as well. FarmStay US.com, while not focused only on health, shows where you can stay on farms and help with farm chores.

🍃 **Enroll in a nature-focused camp for a day, week, or summer.**
The American Camp Association offers a guide and online database at Find.ACACamps.org of more than 2,400 accredited camps, including camps focused on providing experiences in the natural world. True, many camps are now tech-dominated, and too many have disappeared altogether. But ACA camps are responsible for preserving as many as 170,000 acres of undeveloped land, an area 30,000 acres larger than Zion National Park. Among the trends: a gradual increase in camp participation, with day camps (some in urban areas) increasing in number faster than resident camps. Family-oriented camps are also increasingly popular, and that is associated with another growing subset of camps that address the challenges and capacities of young people with medical disorders. Also, camps aren't only for kids anymore. At Campgrounded.org, for example, you can learn about summer camps for adults.

🍂 **Look into outdoor therapy and wilderness programs.**

Casting for Recovery, founded in 1966, is a nonprofit that teaches fly-casting and offers fishing retreats to breast-cancer survivors. Among the goals: physical and emotional benefits, with a focus on wellness and empowerment, while enjoying beautiful surroundings and the healing force of nature. Many wilderness therapy programs focus on addiction and behavioral issues. The Outdoor Behavioral Healthcare Council is also a resource for information about nature-based camps and other outdoor therapy for troubled teens. The council promotes program standards, ethics, and risk management and facilitates research on the effectiveness of wilderness programs. The Addiction Recovery Guide offers an online guide to outdoor therapy for drug and alcohol addiction recovery.

GO ON YOUR OWN NATURE RETREAT FOR MENTAL HEALTH

As with using nature experiences to help improve physical health, applications to mental health should augment other therapies, if those are needed. Psychotherapist and ecopsychologist Patricia Hasbach, PhD, in the book *Ecopsychology*, describes ecotherapy as enlarging "the traditional scope of treatment to include the human-nature relationship." She makes the assumption that no matter how removed a client seems from direct experience of nature in their lives, the *need* to connect is there. Some mental health professionals apply nature therapy indirectly. Working with troubled teenagers in Sacramento, California, psychiatrist Claude Arnet takes them for a walk along the Sacramento River before a session, which he says helps open them to the therapy. "Ecotherapy recognizes that the outer world and our inner world are intimately connected," he says. Hasbach often suggests what she calls "the Experience the Special Place

Assignment," which she says families can do on their own. Similar to Jon Young's "Sit Spot," the concept emphasizes mindfulness:

🍃 **Select a special place outdoors that you feel nurtures mental health.**
Select a place outdoors that you will visit for one month—several times each week, at various times of the day, and in various weather conditions. Be present to this place for at least a half hour per visit. Find a comfortable spot and sit quietly.

🍃 **Slow the mind and the breath as you reflect on these questions:**
How do you feel in this place, and what state of mind arises? What is the nature of your relationship to this place? What relationships do you recognize in this place? What physical sensations do you notice when you are here? What do you feel compelled to write about in your journal when you are here? What are you curious about regarding this place? Over time, this exercise can foster "a gradual deepening of sensitivity, heightened sensory perception, and a sense of embeddedness and belonging," says Hasbach.

The Wellness Walk

••••••••••••••••••••••••••••••••

Every culture brings its own special knowledge to tapping the natural world for health. Jose Gonzalez grew up with his grandparents in Mexico. His family raised corn and peanuts, and his grandfather taught him to ride a horse. He remembers going on nature walks with his entire family.

"My grandparents would share their knowledge of plants and animals. Instead of the typical naturalist identification—that's a tree and here's its name—my elders knew more about how it could be used," he says. "Our nature walks were 'nature health walks' or wellness walks. My grandparents would smell a specific plant and say, 'This reminds me of making tea.' My uncle would say, 'This is good for the eyes. This is good for the kidneys.'"

When Jose was nine, his parents moved to the United States. He went on to get a degree in education, and founded Latino Outdoors, which works to reconnect young Latinos to the nature traditions of their grandparents, and promote the connections between health, history, and the natural world. "My community can talk about their own migration by talking about the birds and the butterflies. The stories of the migrating birds are the stories of my community."

BE A WEATHER WARRIOR

·····················

There's no such thing as bad weather, just bad clothing." So the saying goes. Well, of course there's such a thing as bad weather. Think Hurricane Sandy. But there's no reason to let plain old inclement weather keep you inside, once you know how to stay safe and relatively comfortable. (A hiking buddy of mine always says on the day before we hike, "If we're lucky, we'll have bad weather tomorrow." By that, he means the hike will be more interesting.) On most days, preparation and imaginative activities can get all of us outside. If we're lucky, the weather will be . . . interesting. And it can be another way of knowing the natural world.

Activities and Safety Tips for Cold, Wet, and Snowy Weather

● **Go outside for health.**

Students in all-weather schools in Scandinavia have fewer colds and are less likely to get the flu. So Kari Svenneby, a Norwegian living in Toronto and founder of Active Kids Club, makes it a point to get her students outdoors on most days. Her top tips for dressing for cold-weather adventure: wear thermal underwear (preferably wool) and dress in layers.

❧ Adopt the "sunny day rule."

One father suggests this approach: "If it's a beautiful day, there's no excuse for growing roots on the sofas. Outside with you, I tell them. Go! Go build something!" When it rains, show your kids the joys of puddle stomping, ditch damming, leaf boating.

❧ Learn about the secret lives of snowflakes.

If you live in an area that gets snow, encourage your child to take up snowflake-watching as a winter hobby. Each snowflake, like each child, is unique. Crystals of clear ice, they are not, by the way, pure white. They reflect the winter sky or other surroundings, and can resemble stars, flowers, ferns, and other designs of nature. Carry a low-cost fold-up magnifier and a snowflake field guide. Collect snowflakes by chilling sheets of black paper in a freezer, and use them to catch falling flakes; they won't melt on cold paper. Recommended books: *The Secret Life of a Snowflake* and *Field Guide to Snowflakes*, which compares the "underappreciated recreation" of snowflake-watching to bird-watching.

❧ Build an igloo, snow fort, or snow cave.

Kids or families can pack buckets, plastic storage boxes, or other easy-to-fill containers with moist snow to make bricks. Give children an old ruler or yardstick to separate the sides of the brick from the container. A safe height for walls is about four feet, depending on the size of the children. You and your kids can also use trash cans as molds for extra-large snow bricks. Want a roof? Cover the fort with a roof of branches or evergreen boughs. Using proper safety precautions, older kids and adults can graduate to building igloos and other enclosed snow structures. BoysLife.org offers igloo-construction tips, and Treehugger.com shows how to fashion a variation called a quinzee (or quinzhee, an Athabascan word), or a freeform snow-dome cave.

❧ Go sledding, snow tubing, or tobogganing.

For sledding, traditional wood sleds with metal runners have gradually given way to one-piece plastic sleds and disks, or inflatable snow tubes or toboggans. You and your kids, or kids by themselves, can also create a makeshift sled out of flattened cardboard or a trash bag. For an extra-fast DIY sled, combine both materials (instructions at Instructables.com). Be safe. Look for a slope that is treeless, rockless, and roadless. Unfortunately, some municipalities now prohibit sledding because of liability concerns, so check local regulations.

Try snowshoeing, and make your own.

Commercial snowshoes (no lessons or lift tickets required) are available in many sizes. And for emergencies, Rick Stafford, inventor and outdoorsman, introduced a unique design for inflatable snowshoes called Airlite. Light and packable, they can save lives in unexpected blizzards. You and your kids can make your own. BoysLife.org shows how to make DIY snowshoes out of rope and flexible CPVC piping. Or create rudimentary snowshoes out of rope, plywood, or cardboard. A suggested special effect to excite the neighbors: make DIY snowshoes in the shape of bear or Bigfoot tracks.

Study a winter tree; tap a spring maple.

In many parts of the country, nature centers and farms invite families to tap maple trees and collect the sap for syrup. Look for maple-tapping family festivals and other events in your region. For example, the Red Tricycle website lists events in the Chicago area. With your kids, learn how these trees store starch for the winter and turn it into sugar in the early spring. Encourage youngsters to study, draw, and photograph maples and other species of trees as they change through the seasons.

Play prehistoric hockey.

If your family has access to a frozen pond, play ice hockey. If you're wary about kids strapping blades to their feet and using hockey sticks, suggest miaciolka, a game from Belarus, described by Belarusguide.com as "prehistoric hockey." Substituting brooms for sticks and pieces of ice for pucks, this game is simple and can accommodate a large number of players. No one should ever play ice hockey on frozen rivers or, obviously, thin ice. Be safe. If in doubt, don't. Adult presence preferred.

Keep an instant-snowman kit handy.
Get your family ready for the next snowfall by assembling an instant-snowman (or snow-woman) kit. For eyes, kids can collect rocks and buttons and paint them black. Add a knit cap (or black top hat made from construction paper), scarf, and mittens. Store these items in a bucket, handy for hauling snow. For a nose, use a carrot. Include branches, twigs, evergreen boughs, and other items. Why stop with *snowmo sapiens*? Your family can create snow bears, beavers, rabbits, or other animals.

Hold a snow angel fashion show.
Many parents recall making snow angels — lying in the snow, spreading arms and legs to make the pattern of wings. Here's a twist for your kids. Give each snow angel a fashion makeover and turn them into superheroes — or wild animals. "Fill plastic squirt bottles with water and add a few drops of food coloring to each," suggests Susan Sachs Lipman, author of *Fed Up with Frenzy*. "Head outside, make snow angels, and then paint clothes or faces on them with the colored water."

Track down the last teddy bear in the woods.
No snow? No problem. Author Sara St. Antoine suggests this fun way to get small kids out on a cold day: Secretly hide a dozen or so of their stuffed animals in your yard — in trees and shrubs, on top of logs and behind rocks. Dress children in warm clothes and outfit them with binoculars. Now tell them it's time to go on a wild animal safari. They'll be surprised and delighted to find their beloved stuffed animals in unfamiliar places.

Dress for winter success.
The American Academy of Pediatrics offers the following tips to keep children warm and safe outside on a cold winter day: Dress

infants and children in several thin layers; generally, dress older babies and young children in one more layer of clothing than an adult would wear in similar weather; use moisture-wicking fabrics and clothing geared to the activity or sport; choose durable, flexible, water-absorbent wool over cotton; bring warm boots, gloves or mittens, and a hat; choose clothing that fits well but does not restrict movement; the same is true for footwear. Shoes or boots that constrict blood flow can cause feet to become colder. Slightly larger sizes will allow for an extra pair of socks.

🍂 **In every season, avoid overexposure.**
Spend more time outdoors, but protect your kids (and yourself) from hypothermia, frostbite, and sunburn. Set reasonable time limits, come inside periodically to warm up, and use sunscreen. Definitely use sunscreen. Skin can still burn in winter, especially on days when sun reflects off snow. People perspire in winter as well as summer, so stay hydrated. Drink plenty of water, herbal tea, hot cocoa, and low-sugar fruit juices rich in vitamin C, which may help prevent winter colds and flu.

Activities and Safety Tips for Very Hot Weather

🍂 **Be sun safe.**
We all need vitamin D, and in fact many people get too little of it from their food or from the sun. But protecting our children and ourselves from too much sun is also important. The American Academy of Dermatology (AAD) recommends that all kids—regardless of their skin tone—wear sunscreen with an SPF of 30 or higher. In addition to sunscreen, children should wear sunglasses and hats. Infants and toddlers are particularly vulnerable to heat.

🍃 Make shade while the sun shines.

Install a sun umbrella or a marine fabric sun shade over a patio, part of the yard, or other play areas. For the long haul, plant fast-growing trees for shade, or make good use of the ones you have. One study found trees planted on the south or west side of homes in Sacramento, California, saved homeowners about $25 a year—a small savings in the short run, but a sizable reduction of carbon emissions in the long term, when looking at the big picture. In the meantime, look forward to a lower sunburn rate.

🍃 Build a fort, lean-to, tree house, or playhouse for shade and shelter.

Natural shelters built for or preferably by kids can be as complex as a small shack or playhouse or as simple as a blanket rigged on a rope tied to two trees. They're cool. Sometimes literally. (And they come in handy during snowstorms, too.) Outdoor shelters help protect kids from sunburn and encourage them to spend more time outside.

🍃 Be tick safe.

The Centers for Disease Control (CDC) offers tips for dressing for tick protection. Among them: When hiking in likely areas for ticks (moist and humid, particularly in or near woods or grassy areas), walk in the center of trails; use products containing permethrin to treat boots, clothing, and camping gear; use a repellent with DEET on the skin. Also, tuck pant cuffs into socks and boots to protect against ticks, and wear light-colored clothing so you can see any ticks. Shower soon after being outdoors, and know how to check the body (yours and your child's) for ticks. The CDC also offers information about removing ticks and creating outdoor tick-safe zones. Be aware that repellents can be toxic to people. The American Academy of Pediatrics provides detailed information about how to use these insect repellents safely.

◗ Spray a rainbow.

Hot weather offers kids and adults a great excuse to get wet. Encourage your toddlers to paint with water, stomp on a watery surface, or you can punch holes in an old hose to create a kid sprinkler. Parents.com magazine offers a list of water-play ideas, including one called Spray of Light—using a spray bottle or hose to water outdoor plants while watching for rainbows that appear in the mist.

◗ Go summer sledding or sandboarding.

If you live somewhere close to sand dunes, or are planning a vacation to such a place, your kids and teenagers can experiment with snowboarding's lesser-known cousin: sandboarding. Commercial sandboards are pretty much just like snowboards, except they're made with tougher material. Rent before you buy. Your kids can also use a big piece of cardboard to sled down a grassy hill, or they can do as East Timor children do and slide down a grassy hill on a large palm frond.

◗ Learn how plants breathe.

On a sunny day, place a Ziploc bag over a leafy part of a plant and zip it as far closed as possible. Wait twenty minutes and come back to see the respiration moisture that's accumulated inside the bag. Help your kids experiment with different kinds of plants to detect any difference. Education.com advises: "This simple activity will provide your kid with visual proof that plants are producing the oxygen we need to survive."

THE INDOOR EXPEDITION: FOR WHEN YOU CAN'T GO OUTSIDE

Nature needn't stop at your front door. When it's just too hot or cold, or if family members are unable to leave the home for health reasons, you and your kids can still connect with the natural world.

🍃 **Set up a world-watching window.**

Enjoy moon watching, stargazing, cloudspotting, bird-watching, and more, from indoors. Keep handy: a nature notebook, field guides for birds and stars, binoculars, a telescope, a digital camera with a telephoto lens, and maybe even a sound recorder to capture the sounds of the natural world.

🍃 **Keep an indoor/outdoor illustrated journal.**

Encourage your kids to set up a table next to a window, with art supplies. Paint or draw the life and natural elements beyond the glass. In her book *The Nature Connection*, naturalist and artist Clare Walker Leslie writes, "I often draw little landscapes in places where nature seems hard to find—out a classroom window, along a highway, or outside a hotel. Do you remember 'Where's Waldo?' If you look, you'll be surprised at what you might find."

🍃 **Create a cold-weather sculpture from nature.**

Help your child fill a Bundt cake pan or similar container with water. Let your kids place leaves and other natural items inside it, put it in the freezer, unmold, and hang it outside with string on a cold day. Recommended book: *Get Outside Guide*.

🍃 **Start a windowsill garden.**

No matter how cold or hot it is, you and your kids can start a simple indoor garden using an egg, milk, or juice carton (cut these in half). Fill the carton partway with soil, place on a windowsill or other sunny spot, water, and see what grows. Recommended book: *I Love Dirt*.

🌱 **Grow a radish inside a balloon.**

Put a funnel in the neck of a clear balloon and pour in a half cup of dirt. Then add a quarter cup of water and a few radish seeds. Blow the balloon up, tie it off, and hang it in a window where it will get ample sunlight. The balloon serves as a greenhouse, and the radish will grow quickly. More information at Education.com.

🌱 **Go on an insect safari in your home.**

Your children may be surprised (and pleasantly grossed out) to discover just how many species of bugs are living in the nooks and crannies of your house or apartment. To identify secret roommates, and make friends and influence enemies, consult a regional insect site, or find an online resource, such as Yourwidlife.org or the Finding Urban Nature section of NationalGeographic.com.

🌱 **Raise a praying mantis.**

Mantises are among the strangest and most fascinating insects. Their eggs can be acquired from online retailers, and they're fairly easy to raise. KeepingInsects.com offers this advice, and more: Keep a mantis in a terrarium or cage with substrate that can absorb water, such as tissue paper, potting earth, pieces of bark, or sand. This helps keep the humidity more constant. Place branches or twigs for the mantis to climb; and occasionally feed it live insects (you can offer it the food with tweezers). Fair warning: If you have both male and female praying mantises, they may not be the best domestic role models.

🌱 **Keep insect-eating plants.**

Carnivorous plants can add excitement to your family's indoor garden. *Better Homes & Gardens* advises: "Insect-eating plants need high humidity, bright (but not direct) light, and a special growing medium that is moist and acidic." Do not feed your insect-eating plants hamburger or other meats (too much protein); they prefer flies and other small insects. They also attract neighborhood kids. Should your carnivorous plant ever say, "Feed me," put it outside. More information at BHG.com.

🌿 Build a houseplant tree house.

While your family is dreaming about warmer days, show your kids how to build a houseplant tree house—but let them do the heavy lifting—using small sticks, tongue depressors, or Popsicle sticks. Then assemble the items in a favorite ficus or other large potted plant. This miniature can serve as a blueprint for building a full-scale tree fort when spring arrives. More detailed instructions for houseplant tree houses can be found at ImagineChildhood.com.

🌿 Create a tabletop biosphere.

Turn a jar into a self-sustaining closed ecosystem. Among the ingredients to include: hornwort (a plant), freshwater shrimp, snails, tap water dechlorinator, freshwater nutrient minerals, pond water (containing small, shrimplike invertebrates). Fill the jar almost to the top with dechlorinated water and seal. Full instructions are available at Makezine.com.

🌿 Make a worm terrarium.

No need to buy an expensive glass tank. Wash out a standard two-liter soda bottle and fill it with alternating layers of sand, dirt, and leaves. Introduce worms, and watch as they blend the layers together.

🌿 Set up an aquarium.

Freshwater aquariums need careful preparation to set up, but they are easier to maintain than saltwater aquariums. Pick a twenty- to fifty-five-gallon tank, and buy other essentials like gravel or sand, a filter, water plants, decorations, a water dechlorinator, and, of course, fish. Recommended book: Animal Planet's *Your First Aquarium*.

🌿 Raise a butterfly indoors.

Collect a butterfly egg by trimming off the section of plant it's attached to. Put this clipping in a small, airtight container and wait three to seven days for the egg to hatch. Once the caterpillar starts to grow, transfer it to a larger plastic container with fresh foliage. Do not perforate the lid. Open the container daily to clean out the droppings and dead leaves. When the caterpillar is fully grown, add a stick to the container. The caterpillar will attach to it and form a chrysalis. Cut a hole in the lid to hold the stick vertically and wait for the butterfly to emerge—and then release it into the wild. Recommended books: *Nature's Notes* and *Bumper Book of Nature*.

Be a Weather Detective

🌿 **Become an extreme-weather expert.**
Some folks put themselves in harm's way as storm-chasers in search of tornadoes; that's a dangerous endeavor, but it's amazing how much drama you can see and experience from your own neighborhood. Of course, put safety first. The Yahoo Group, Severe Weather Watchers (find it on Groups.Yahoo.com) offers advice and a place to share meteorological stories, photographs, or website links. You can also post on Pinterest Weather Watcher Extreme. Recommended book for kids: *National Geographic Kids Everything Weather: Facts, Photos, and Fun That Will Blow You Away.*

🌿 **Take up cloudspotting.**
Observe the different patterns and kinds of clouds. Gavin Pretor-Pinney launched the Cloud Appreciation Society in 2004. In *The Cloudspotter's Guide* he expresses his passion for clouds, with a sense of humor: "At [t]he Cloud Appreciation Society we love clouds, we're not ashamed to say it and we've had enough of people moaning about them." The society's manifesto makes a stand against "the banality of 'blue-sky thinking.'" Cloudspotting is available to anyone, and it's great for a child or adult in a hospital bed, or for someone with a disability that prevents them from going outdoors.

🍃 Learn to use nature's secret code to predict the weather.

Natural occurrences can be used to predict the weather. According to one folktale, you and your kids can predict harsh weather by counting the pattern and number of the hairs on a wooly bear caterpillar (but who has the time?). It's probably not true. At least not for practical purposes. Other sayings about the weather, though, turn out to be accurate. Among them: Rainbow in the morning gives you fair warning; clear moon, frost soon; the higher the clouds, the finer the weather; red sky at night, sailors delight; red sky in morning, sailors take warning. Learn more online at OldFarmersAlmanac.com. Make a rain gauge, a barometer, or weather vane, or full backyard or rooftop weather station.

🍃 Use nature to forecast the weather.

Farmers rely on it. Land forms are shaped by it. Even some sea creatures (and certainly land creatures) depend on rainwater for their survival. Watch and measure local rainfall by creating a simple rain gauge, otherwise known as a udometer, pluviometer, or an ombrometer, as explained by Scholastic Weather Watch on Scholastic's website, which offers snow gauges and other weather activities, too. Help your child make a barometer or weather vane. Or go all the way and build a weather station, plans courtesy of the National Oceanic and Atmospheric Administration (NOAA).

🍃 Go fly a kite.

Flying a kite encourages us to look up, be active, and understand wind patterns. Get your children started with kite flying by helping them with a kit or by making a DIY kite out of paper, sticks, and string. National Geographic Kids offers online plans for a kite. Kites were invented in China, and the first kites may have been made of leaves. And humans aren't the only animals who appreciate kites. Some species of spider create "kites" out of spider silk to carry them on the wind. Suggested books: *The Complete Book of Kites and Kite Flying.*

Why We All Need Sunshine for Health

∙∙∙∙∙∙∙∙∙∙∙∙∙∙∙∙∙∙∙∙∙∙∙∙∙∙∙∙∙∙∙∙∙∙∙∙∙∙∙

The threat of melanoma is serious and growing. Precautions should be taken. But avoiding the sun too much exacts its own price. Health-care providers warn that a worldwide increase of vitamin D deficiency is linked to increased risk of death from cardiovascular disease, cognitive impairment in older adults, severe asthma in children, and cancer. Vitamin D can be absorbed in our diet from some fish or fish liver oils, egg yolks, and other foods, though we mainly get it from the sun.

Myopia—more often called nearsightedness or shortsightedness—is also reaching epidemic proportions. In the United States and Europe, the rate of nearsightedness among young adults has doubled in the past half century. In Seoul, South Korea, a staggering 96.5 percent of nineteen-year-old men are myopic. Eyeglasses help, but myopia can increase the chances of retinal detachment, cataracts, glaucoma, and blindness. The science journal *Nature* reports that scientists are "challenging old ideas that myopia is the domain of the bookish child and are instead coalescing around a new notion: that spending too long indoors is placing children at risk." Kathryn Rose, head of orthoptics at the University of Technology, Sydney, told the journal, "We're really trying to give this message now that children need to spend more time outside."

Here's another health incentive to head outdoors, and also to design our homes, schools, offices, workplaces, and health-care facilities to make better use of natural light. As John Denver advised, sunshine on our shoulders makes us happy. "Bright light suppresses daytime melatonin production and normalizes circadian rhythms," writes Kathi J. Kemper, MD, in her book *Mental Health, Naturally: The Family Guide to Holistic Care for a Healthy Mind and Body*, published by the American Academy of Pediatrics. "Restoring internal rhythms (the normal daily variations in sleepiness, appetite, activity, temperature, blood pressure, and other physiologic functions) promotes mental and physical health," she adds. "Several studies suggest that . . . morning light can help with sleep, day-night activity patterns, and agitated behavior."

But what about the dark side of sunshine? "Anything done to excess can be hazardous," Kemper says. Wear sunscreen and hats. Create shady areas, preferably by planting trees around the house and neighborhood. Shaded sunlight works, too. Kemper recommends that people get "at least fifteen to thirty minutes of sunshine or bright light daily." People who suffer from seasonal affective disorder may need even more time outside.

Other Voices

"Weather is part of our third-grade curriculum. We study the Beaufort wind scale, cloud types, and then pretend a storm might be coming. The students are provided with a tarp, a few small sections of rope, and access to trees. Teamwork, problem solving, critical thinking, creativity, engineering . . . they *always* want more time."

—Jennifer Davies, Avon, Indiana

"Pile up snow, throw some shovels down near the kids and walk away."

—Jimmy Fox, Fairbanks, Alaska

"When we take kids to the doctor, there is always a question on the form asking how many hours of screen time your child gets each day—it's an expectation. There is nothing about how many hours they spend outside—no expectation. Clearly the approach needs to change!"

—Linda Nagel Madson, Minneapolis, Minnesota

"Kids are being diagnosed with anxiety, depression, ADHD, irritable bowel syndrome and migraine headaches at all-time high rates. Whatever labels we want to use, the message is clear—our children are suffering from stress. I worry about our medical systems' ineffective and (at times) dangerous 'one ill–one pill' approach. My point here is about prevention. Getting kids back into nature is a key part of the solution to keeping kids healthy and truly creating wellness."

—Lawrence Rosen, MD, past chair of the
American Academy of Pediatrics
Section on Integrative Medicine

"If we stress a connection to the natural environment, we can lessen the lifelong effects of a stressful childhood including depression, obesity, behavior problems, drug use and risk-taking behavior . . . A walk in the woods, climbing a tree or patiently watching a fish rise to a dry fly will not solve everything, but it could go a long way to bring things into a more positive, hopeful perspective."

—Mary Brown, MD, Bend, Oregon,
past member of the board of directors,
American Academy of Pediatrics

Part 7

. . . .

The School of Nature

"We do not organize education the way we sense the world. If we did, we would have departments of Sky, Landscapes, Water, Wind, Sounds, Time, Seashores, Swamps, and Rivers."

—DAVID ORR,
AUTHOR OF *ECOLOGICAL LITERACY*

"Nature-study cultivates in the child a love of the beautiful . . . a perception of color, form, and music . . . But more than all, nature-study gives the child a sense of companionship with life out-of-doors and an abiding love of nature."

—ANNA BOTSFORD COMSTOCK,
HANDBOOK OF NATURE STUDY,
ORIGINAL COPYRIGHT 1911

BE A NATURAL TEACHER,
AT HOME AND AT SCHOOL

. . . .

A natural teacher is anyone who uses the power of nature as a tool for education or as an environment for learning—not only about nature, but about any subject.

Parents, grandparents, grandfriends, uncles, aunts, the good people who offer outdoor programs, park rangers, citizen naturalists, the woman with the great garden who lives down the street and invites the kids over—they can all be natural teachers.

So can environmental educators, and the art, science, or language teachers who insist on taking their students outdoors to learn in nature—to draw or study the life in the creek at the end of the schoolyard or to write poetry under the trees. And so can the principals, superintendents, and school board members who support them.

Natural teaching begins in the backyard, the community garden, a roof garden, a park, and follows a trail to the school garden, the classroom, and into the future.

Demand may grow quickly. When Anna Kemp's son was starting school, she heard about a nature-based kindergarten. She wanted that for her child. "Clearly, the promise of nature kindergarten made instinctive sense to a lot of parents," she wrote in January 2015 in the *Times Colonist* of Victoria, British Columbia. "On sign-up day, I had planned to get up at 4 a.m. to be first in line. However, when I drove by the school the day before, parents were already camped out. By 9 p.m., twelve hours before the school opened, the twenty spots in the region's first nature kindergarten were spoken for."

An increasing number of homeschoolers, nature preschools, and independent primary and secondary schools are incorporating nature experience into learning (not only learning *about* nature, but using natural habitat as a learning environment for a wide range of subjects). Forward-thinking public schools are adopting the methods as well. With good reason. The research base is growing.

One recent study, from Spain, indicates that green spaces, especially at schools, are linked to improved cognitive development in children, including in memory and a reduction in inattentiveness, as surrounding greenness increased.

Learning in nature has long been associated with better cognitive functioning. Now comes word of recent research to underscore that link, related to testing. A six-year study of 905 public elementary schools in Massachusetts reported higher scores on standardized testing in English and math in schools that incorporated more nature. Similarly, preliminary results from a yet-to-be-published ten-year University of Illinois study of over 500 Chicago schools show similar findings, especially for students with the greatest educational needs.

Based on that study, the researchers suggest that greening our schools may be one of the most cost-effective ways to raise student test scores.

IGNITE NATURAL LEARNING AT HOME AND SCHOOL

Most of the actions recommended in previous sections of this book can be described as learning activities and experiences. But here are a few specific ideas that parents can apply to home and family, and teachers can use at school.

🍃 Read about nature together or encourage solo reading outdoors.

Reading with your child or grandchild outside can soothe the soul, theirs and yours. Solitary reading outdoors offers special resonance, perhaps because our senses are more stimulated under a tree than next to a TV. "My child loves to read challenging works of literature," says Margaret Lamar of San Antonio, Texas. "He creates entire imaginary worlds from what he reads, and he lives out those characters in dramatic play with his brother as they run around outdoors." Read books that inspire people, young or old, to explore nature, or ones specific to natural history—especially the natural history of your own backyard, city, and bioregion.

🍃 Make a root viewer to show how plant roots work.

While we know that roots help plants absorb water and nutrients from the soil, they may be more complex than you think. Plant roots use their hairs to feel around the soil. Research from the UK's John Innes Centre recently showed just how: The hairs absorb nutrients by releasing a unique protein at their tips. When the hairs hit rocks or other obstacles, they stop taking up nutrients, which in turn signals the root to find another path and start creating protein again. Fill clear cups or bottles about four-fifths full with dirt. Plant a seed or two in each cup, close to the edge. Place near a sun source. Water, and observe as roots form and plants sprout. If you get really carried away with this project, you could be like the UK's Joe Atherton, who grows his World Record–setting carrots (carrots are roots) in twenty-one-foot-long plastic tubes. See these veggie-monsters at CarrotMuseum.co.uk. Recommended book: *Fed Up with Frenzy*.

🍃 Study bird behavior to demonstrate predicting, observing, and analyzing.

An earlier chapter mentioned learning to call birds and to understand bird language. Those are good activities for natural learning. So is another activity, suggested by nature educator Herb Broda.

"Many common birds such as blue jays, English sparrows and starlings relish table scraps," he says. "To test bird feed color preference, cooked macaroni is offered as food. Add natural food coloring (think beet juice, carrot juice, blueberry juice, etc.) to color cooked macaroni and offer birds their choice of blue, orange, pink or uncolored food. Have kids generate predictions about how birds will react to the colored food."

🌿 **Plant rainbow seeds; experience the shades of green.**
Ask your child, grandchild, or students to collect small samples of differing shades of green that they find in the lawn, garden, park, or school ground. Ask them to find five to fifteen different shades of green. Give each child a cardboard strip. "I slice up old manila file folders into two-inch-wide strips," says Broda. "Then, place a piece of masking tape, sticky side up, along the entire length of the strip. Have your child look carefully at the collected samples and arrange them on the cardboard strip from lightest to darkest. It works especially well if you limit the search area to a small space," Broda advises. "Emphasize that although it's okay to collect in our garden, we shouldn't sample anywhere else unless we have special permission." Suggested book: *Acclimatizing.* The beautiful book *Planting a Rainbow* shows children the variety of colors that can be found in a garden, provides the names of especially colorful and familiar plants, and helps them develop attention to detail. Plant some seeds and watch the illustrations in the book appear as flowers in your garden.

🌿 **Hold a scavenger hunt as a teaching activity.**
Scavenger hunts need no preparation or materials. They can reenergize flagging attention and be related to concepts being taught in school. Here are a few examples: Ask kids to use their senses to find a soft object, something that makes a sound, something that smells good, something sticky, something prickly. Or gather an item for each letter of the alphabet. Find rectangles in nature (or

circles, squares, triangles). Look for a bird nest, squirrel nest, or insect home (be sure to stress that homes not be disturbed). Find ten examples of weathering or camouflage. Find something funny, something sad, something tired, something old, something young. Find things that will not be here next year, next month, tomorrow. Scavenger Hunt Guru offers a good list for urban scavenger hunts for, among other evidence of nature, flowers growing from sidewalk cracks, the smallest living thing, and the sounds of wild animals in the city. Nature Rocks suggests a seed hunt. Encourage kids to bring them home or to school, and see what grows. To further facilitate scavenger hunts, obtain Leopold Exploration Cards from the Aldo Leopold Foundation in Baraboo, Wisconsin. Recommended books: *Moving the Classroom Outdoors* and *In Accord with Nature*.

🌿 **Keep a Wonder Bowl at home or in the classroom.**
Kids, particularly the younger ones, like to fill their pockets with natural wonders — acorns, rocks, mushrooms. "My mom got tired of washing clothes and finding these treasures in the bottom of the washer or disintegrated through the dryer," Liz Baird, who started Take a Child Outside Week, recalls. "So she came up with 'Liz's Wonder Bowl.' The idea was that I could empty my pockets into the bowl. I could still enjoy my treasures, and try to find out what things were, and not cause trouble with the laundry." Wonder Bowls are also useful in classrooms, particularly in the early grades. In addition to facilitating the child's desire to hunt and gather, a Wonder Bowl is a good way to collect items for show-and-tell and further study. To polish prized stones, use an inexpensive rock tumbler. (The children's television icon Fred Rogers had one of his own.) Gather ye pebbles while ye may.

🌿 **To demonstrate flow and trajectory, do Poohsticks.**
For home or school, nature educator Herb Broda suggests an activity that comes directly from *The House at Pooh Corner* by A. A. Milne. The perfect setting is a small bridge over a slowly flowing stream, although the activity could be done from the creek

bank if there is no bridge nearby. The activity is simple: two or more players drop their sticks at the same time from the upstream side of the bridge. The challenge is to see whose stick first appears on the other side of the bridge. It's amazing how a simple challenge like this can engage children and adults for quite a long time. "Of course you can 'schoolify' the activity by talking about rate of flow or stick trajectory," says Broda. "But this really is an activity to do just for fun—to share a moment of exuberance while walking with a child."

For a teachable moment that kids won't forget, go for gross.

Maria Rodale of Rodale, Inc., offers wise advice: "Look for scat. We have a fox that loves to mark its territory by pooping right in the middle of the driveway. What kid doesn't love to talk about poop? Every kid should know the difference between deer poop and rabbit poop and other kinds of poop. The wild animal poop list is endless . . . and endlessly fascinating." And don't miss out on owl pellets, which you can find and dissect. Owls mostly eat rodents, but they can't digest their bones and fur. About ten hours after a meal, an owl will regurgitate (barf) a fur and bone "pellet" that can be dissected like gross little treasure chests. Find a tree where an owl is likely to live (tall, close to an open field, with bird poop on the trunk), and search around the base for pellets. You'll be amazed. Suggested book: *The Bumper Book of Nature*.

The Nature-Rich School:
How Parents and Teachers Can
Support One Another as Natural Teachers

🍃 **Learn more about the benefits of
nature-based education.**

Resources include: *Green Teacher* magazine, available in English,
Spanish, and French, and the *Learning with Nature Idea Book*, published by the Arbor Day Foundation.

🍃 **Choose, support, or help start a nature-based
school.**

If you can find a good nature preschool, enroll your child and support that school with your time and money. Later, favor public K–12
schools that place community and direct experience in nature at
the center of the curriculum. Montessori and Waldorf schools have
a long history of support for direct-experience learning, often in
natural settings. Many homeschoolers are creating nature-rich
learning environments.

🍃 **As a parent or teacher, encourage an
"all-weather" policy.**

In Finland, which is consistently near the top of the list in math
and science testing (the United States is significantly lower on the
list), students spend much of the day outdoors — no matter how
cold the temperature.

🍃 **Green the schoolyard.**

To get started, download the U.S. Fish and Wildlife Service's
Schoolyard Habitat Project Guide. Tap the knowledge of such programs as Evergreen in Canada, and the Natural Learning Initiative
in the United States. Also, see a worldwide list of schoolyard greening organizations, including ones in Canada, Norway, Sweden, the
United Kingdom, and the United States.

🍃 Help start a school garden.

Read more about the many benefits of school gardens, and learn about school gardening projects at KidsGardening.org. Sensory gardens use plant life, scented herbs, smooth river rocks, and other natural elements to stimulate the five basic senses and other, lesser-known vestibular, proprioceptive, and kinesthetic senses, among others. These gardens (as all school gardens should be) are designed for universal access—meaning for students with or without cognitive or physical disabilities.

🍃 Provide training in the value and management of natural risk.

Teachers, play leaders (or "playworkers" as they're called in the UK), and parents who supervise groups of children need regular training in play leadership. "Such training has been successful in adventure playgrounds, and limited numbers of forest schools, zoos, child development centers, children's museums and expanding integrated natural/built playgrounds at schools and parks," says international play expert Joe Frost. Common sense helps. But up-to-date knowledge about play and risk is essential.

🍃 Work with local organizations to create nature gyms in schoolyards and parks.

Pull up the asphalt and create natural play spaces. Consciously use nature for play shade, something to remember when designing backyard and rooftop play spaces. "Trees and shrubs can be placed to provide shade for children and school buildings, reducing sun exposure, urban heat island effects, and interior cooling costs for school buildings," advises environmental planner Sharon Gamson Danks, author of *Asphalt to Ecosystems: Design Ideas for Schoolyard Transformation.*

🌿 **Start a Salmon in the Classroom project
or similar endeavor.**

In Washington State, participating students in more than six hundred schools have received hundreds of hatchery eggs to care for in classrooms. Students learn about life histories and habitat requirements and later release the salmon into streams they have studied. Similar programs exist in other states and countries, including Alaska and Canada. (Some schools, worried about salmonella contamination, don't allow any animals in classrooms. Still, hands-on nature experiences can offer experiences moments, such as "Wash your hands.")

🌿 **Schedule a regular "Dirty Thursday."
Encourage the school to make nature play
a regular part of the day.**

"'Nature play' should be given the respect and time it deserves. This means making it a regular part of the school week and giving it as much importance as everything else," says Ellen Radostitis of Rapperswil, Switzerland. "I found when we named our special 'weekly' trip to our local natural park, the children gave it a certain status and belonging. It was their special time and they made the very best use of it. It was the highlight of their week! Even the parents came on board, were informed of the weekly trips and the name of the day became a part of their week as well (they always had so much dirty laundry to do that evening). Our special day was called simply 'Dirty Thursday.' It was the best part of the whole week because we stayed the whole afternoon and it was 100 percent student directed . . . as it should be."

🌿 **Help create a school eco-club.**

In Cincinnati, Ohio, Outdoor Adventure Clubs offer after-school tutorials in outdoor adventuring to primarily inner-city youths, followed by kayaking, mountain biking, hiking, and rock climbing. OAC has grown from three inner-city high schools to fifteen high schools and middle schools, plus satellite programs, since 2012. Another example: Crenshaw High School Eco-Club, led by the remarkable natural teacher, Bill Vanderberg, has been among the most popular clubs in the predominately African American high school in Los Angeles. In eco-clubs like Vanderberg's, students camp locally and in national parks, and they've also participated in coastal cleanups, nonnative invasive plant removal, and hiking trail maintenance. Past members become mentors for new arrivals. Student grades improve. Lives are changed.

Sponsor a "walkabout camp."

In Chattanooga, Tennessee, the Baylor School's motto is "Making students uncomfortable since 1976." One of the primary ways the school does this is by sponsoring an annual Walkabout. Baylor serves primarily middle and high school students from affluent families, and this activity requires a financial commitment that isn't reachable for most schools without corporate or foundation support. Every summer, students participate in the Walkabout Camp, placing them in challenging outdoor adventures in the United States, Panama, India, and other countries. Many kids resist, but those "are often the ones that come back raving (in a good way) about the experience," according to Baylor Chaplain Dan Scott, "and it changes them forever." More schools are offering summer experiences in the natural world, including some in neighborhoods that are not affluent. More funding could help make more young students, in every kind of community, uncomfortable . . . in a good way.

Make your school a "green haven."

In the public mind, schools are too often associated with stress and even violence. One way to change that perception is to turn them into "green havens," writes Louise Chawla, professor of environmental design, University of Colorado in Boulder, and coeditor of the journal *Children, Youth and Environments*. "Not every family has natural areas around their home or a park down the block, but almost every family sends their children to a school where there is a playground or playing fields." She recommends turning parts of school grounds into gardens, natural habitats for study and play. "Then all children could have a green haven in their lives. A place for calm, peace, and rapt absorption."

The Power of One School to Change a Community

• •

As Celeste Martin, principal of Brookwood Elementary School in Dalton, Georgia, says, "STEM is all the buzz in education these days." (That's the acronym for science, technology, engineering, and mathematics.) The basic idea is to improve competitiveness in technology. Martin and her school have pushed hard to design an interdisciplinary experience that puts an emphasis on outdoor learning experiences.

Here are some examples of the intriguing approaches that Brookwood's students and teachers took, according to a Brookwood report.

- *First grade students* "felt the urgency to help increase the dwindling monarch population." Working with the Tennessee Aquarium in Chattanooga, Tennessee, they researched which plants will best attract the butterflies, created monarch way stations, raised thirty-six monarchs from eggs found in their gardens, tagged twenty-five, and continually documented their observations in their gardens with the USA National Phenology Network. They tested the monarchs for a pesky parasite and released them.

- *Second grade students* hoped to increase positive attitudes toward vegetables. They analyzed plate waste in the cafeteria and came up with a public relations plan first for spinach, the first year's most wasted vegetable, and then for cauliflower.

- *Third grade students* researched compost and its effects on plant growth and organic gardening practices. They shared their findings with the community and promoted composting practices and minimizing the negative effects of pesticides. They also entered a cabbage-growing contest. Their school garden's winner: a forty-two-pound cabbage.

- *Fourth grade students* investigated the turtle population in an adjacent wetland. In collaboration with Dalton State College, they took twenty-four trips to the wetland during the fall to trap turtles. Wearing waders, the students used steel rods and mallets to place sardine-rich trap nets in the water. When the turtles were trapped, students checked to see if they had been previously tagged. They measured the turtles and documented their findings on a data sheet provided by the college, to which they sent their findings.

  The students are also researching water quality and waste in nearby Lakeshore Park and have written and distributed newsletters to tell residents about the diversity of life and the benefits of the park.

- *Fifth grade students* identified and investigated erosion problems around the school for the past two years. The critical area of need was behind their cafeteria. (One might wonder about, well, excess spinach and cauliflower content in the soil.) They also measured the amount of residual soil in the runoff, searched for various erosion control ideas, and proposed a plan for the area's repair, which ultimately saved the school's maintenance department time and effort. "In the process, they discovered the difference between weathering and erosion and how to calculate area and volume of space," according to the report.

- *The fifth graders* also worked to help local residents living in small apartments with no availability of land to garden. The students designed small, recycled containers they called grow boxes, which made it easier for residents to grow vegetables. Over time, they tracked the growth rates in the boxes as they looked for the most effective method to grow local food in small spaces.

Create a Support System for Nature-Based Education

🌿 **Make the case that nature-rich schools help teachers, too.**

Want to help teachers avoid burnout? Canadian researchers report that teachers who get their students — and themselves — outdoors can reignite their own energy and enthusiasm for teaching. Schoolteachers, like parents, receive the same benefits to physical and psychological health and cognitive functioning as children do, when they spend more time outside.

🌿 **Volunteer to help with school nature activities and field trips.**

Parents and other knowledgeable adults — including naturalists, horticulturalists, and gardeners — are an invaluable resource to budget-strapped schools. Retirees can step up to help bring nature into classrooms, create school gardens, give classroom presentations, assist on field trips, and provide many other services to schools. In diverse communities, they can also share cultural knowledge about learning from the natural world. Schools can help by encouraging current volunteers and recruiting more of them.

🌿 **Establish a Parent-Teacher Nature Club.**

Robert Bateman, the renowned Canadian artist, whose paintings often depict wildlife, suggests that teachers and other educators create their own Teacher Nature Clubs to organize weekend hikes and other nature experiences for teachers. Go further: create a Parent-Teacher Nature Club. (Call it the PTN. In fact, your PTA could take the lead and create a PTN.) Such clubs would encourage teachers experienced in the natural world to share their knowledge with less-experienced teachers, and help improve teachers' mental and physical health.

🍃 **Join or support the Natural Teachers Network.**

In many schools and school districts, teachers are not encouraged to take students outdoors, and sometimes they're actively discouraged from doing so. Teachers need one another for mutual support, and they may need to reach far beyond their own schools for that support. The Natural Teachers Network was created by the Children & Nature Network as a way to bring together people who use the natural environment as learning environment, including through the Internet at NaturalTeachers.org.

🍃 **Partner with organizations that support nature-rich education.**

Parents, teachers, and community leaders can work together to tap professional resource programs, among them the North American Association for Environmental Education, Project Learning Tree, and Project WILD, which tie nature-oriented concepts to all major school subjects, requirements, and skill areas. The National Environmental Education and Training Foundation, which is working to green STEM programs (as previously mentioned, STEM is an acronym for the fields of science, technology, engineering, and math), offers a directory of environmental education programs and resources for K–12 teachers, parents, and students. The Center for Ecoliteracy offers a wealth of knowledge. The National Audubon Society, National Wildlife Refuges, the National Park Foundation, and other organizations provide professional development programs and tools correlated to public school curriculum standards.

🍃 **Create nature-based classrooms in the community beyond the school.**

An outdoor classroom is much less expensive than building a new brick-and-mortar wing. Schools, families, businesses, parks, and outdoor organizations can work together to encourage parents to organize a family nature club or join an existing one, introduce students to nature centers and parks, and sponsor overnight trips. They can help develop safe, natural learning environments within walking distance of every school.

The School of a Million Acres

. . . .

A while back, I met with a dozen biology professors at North Carolina Central University. They were deeply concerned about the dramatic deterioration of student knowledge of what's out there: these students can tell you all about the Amazon rain forest, but nothing about the plants and animals of the neighborhoods in which they live.

But nearby nature can become a school of a million acres. In 2010, two Oregon State University researchers, writing in *American Scientist*, brought this into focus." In "The 95 Percent Solution," John H. Falk and Lynn D. Dierking write, "The 'school-first' paradigm is so pervasive that few scientists, educators or policy-makers question it. This despite two important facts: Average Americans spend less than 5 percent of their life in classrooms, and an ever-growing body of evidence demonstrates that most science is learned outside of school."

Falk and Dierking contend that "a major educational advantage enjoyed by the U.S. relative to the rest of the world" is its out-of-school learning landscape, including museums, libraries, zoos, aquariums, national parks, 4-H clubs, scouting, and, I would insert, nature centers, state and local parks, and the nearby nature of our neighborhoods. They add, "The sheer quantity and importance of this science learning landscape lies in plain sight but mostly out of mind." Rather than increasing time in the indoor classroom, "perhaps we should be investing in expanding quality, out-of-school experiences."

Programs that promote out-of-school education can be important allies to natural teachers. For example, Inside the Outdoors, in Orange County, California, serves 150,000 children each year with a nature-based STEM education afterschool program.

Use Your Parent/Teacher Political Power in the Community

🍃 **Exert parent power.**

Parents can demand nature-rich education and have more influence to achieve that goal than they may believe. "School board members, trustees, administrators, and teachers listen to parents big-time," says Tim Grant, editor in chief of the Canada-based journal *Green Teacher*. "Many teachers have said they've made suggestions to principals and received no response, but when the parent makes the same suggestions, things often start to happen" at the national, state, and local levels. Push to enact bills supporting environmental education in the classroom and outdoor experiential learning.

🍃 **Champion the return of recess and other school programs that get kids outside.**

Engage your PTA and other organizations to help bring back recess and physical education—and then go the next step: encourage outdoor exercise and learning. In addition to improving physical and mental health, outdoor time can raise test scores. And now for something completely different: though the approach is still rare, some high schools now allow student athletes to letter in outdoor sports, such as hiking and fishing.

🍃 **Declare an annual Empty Classroom Day.**

In the United Kingdom, schools and organizations pledge to celebrate outdoor learning on Empty Classroom Day on June 19. Ideally, every nation would follow the UK's lead, but your school, school district, community or family doesn't have to wait for a national empty classroom day. Declare it so.

🍃 **Use your parent power to build a bigger constituency for policy change.**

Lobby to bring back recess, to fund field trips and nature-based, experiential learning. Help return natural history to higher education. Work to require universities to teach fundamental natural history, which has been eliminated from the curricula of many research universities, to create degrees and programs that widen the definition of green jobs to include those that connect people to nature, and to fund research on topics involving the relationship between children and nature. Higher education can be a doorway to more career choices, including recreation and service-learning opportunities.

Teach the teachers—and the school board, too.
Many teachers feel inadequately trained to give their students an outdoors experience, and all educators need to know about the benefits to education and the opportunities that already exist. In challenging economic times, community resources may need to be tapped. For example, many wildlife refuges provide professional development programs that have been correlated to public school curriculum standards. But long-term progress will depend on higher education and the incorporation of nature experience into teacher education curricula. The new Nature-Based Early Childhood Certificate program at Antioch University New England includes a business planning course by nature preschool pioneer Ken Finch. And Mary Baldwin College offers an environment-based learning (EBL) graduate program designed specifically for educators.

Honor the Natural Teachers in Schools, Home, and Community

🌿 **PTAs and other groups: help fund natural teachers.**
Along with other public-spirited organizations, conservation groups, and businesses, PTAs and PTSAs can fund nature programs, school gardens, and transportation for field trips. They can sponsor family nature nights at schools and share information on how to create family nature clubs and Kid Watch programs for neighborhood safety. They can also push for positive government and school district policy changes.

🌿 **Create annual Natural Teacher and Nature-Rich School awards.**
PTAs, PTSAs, and other organizations, including businesses, can give awards to those teachers and school administrators who, year after year, get their students outside. Green Ribbon Schools (GRS) is a national awards program that recognizes schools that promote and encourage environmentally friendly learning environments. We need similar awards for the teachers themselves.

🌿 **Provide similar awards for nonprofessional natural teachers.**
Community and education groups can also honor the organizations, parents, and volunteers who help create nature-rich schools or who introduce and maintain nature-rich learning environments in the neighborhoods and at home.

The Uncommon Core:
Help Create a Force for Balance

··

Finding an appropriate mix of technology and reality should be at or near the top of our list of our educational priorities at home; at primary, secondary, and higher education; and in our libraries and every other place of learning.

While educators alone can't change the trajectory of society, the truth is that too many schools and school districts fail to start or support good programs to get kids outside. That's one reason why the regional and state No Child Left Inside campaigns around the country are so important: by building community support, they create a wider constituency for place-based education, bringing social and political heft to the table.

Currently, the force of economics is on the side of technology and standardized efficiency, even for the youngest children. Some preschool chains promote themselves by providing every child with an iPad. One over-the-top—or, actually, under-the-bottom—product is the "Digital iPotty with Activity Seat for iPad" for potty-training infants. It comes with "a built-in iPad stand," and can, according to the manufacturers, be used with "dozens of helpful potty training apps." The *Washington Monthly*'s special report, "The Next Big Test," projects that, thanks to artificial intelligence, the need for standardized testing will fade away, replaced by what proponents call "stealth assessment"—nonstop electronic monitoring of students, employing systems similar to ones grocery chain stores now use to track inventory. Most learning will occur through cutting-edge software "often in the form of video games"—Grand Test Auto, as the *Monthly*'s headline writer calls it. Or at least that's the goal.

Today, children and adults who work and learn in a dominating digital environment expend enormous energy *blocking out* many of the human senses—including ones we don't even know we have—in order to focus narrowly on the screen in front of the eyes. That's the very definition of being less alive. What parent wants his or her child to be less alive? Who among us wants to be less alive?

The point here is not to be against technology, but to find balance. When it comes to shaping the future of our schools, there is no economic force as powerful as the technology industries—with the possible exception of the health industry. Therefore, the only force strong enough to effectively stand up for balance in education and at home will be a social force: parents, teachers, pediatricians, psychologists, and other caring adults who are building a new nature movement.

At home, at school, and even at work, think of experience as a budgeting issue—of time and money. For every dollar invested in the virtual, invest at least another dollar in the natural.

Other Voices

"When starting out as a teacher, I heard Joseph Cornell [founder of Sharing Nature Worldwide] say that keeping children inside one room five days a week is akin to breaking a horse. I'm haunted by that analogy. Our tendency is to keep children in, especially as academic demands only increase. And for discipline or missed work what do we do? Keep them in at recess. Breaking horses."

—*Kelly Keena, PhD, science teacher, Denver, Colorado*

"My son's preschool has made all the difference. It has a large outdoor play yard, vegetable gardens, massive amounts of sand, and an attitude of 'we'll be outside unless it's freezing or pouring rain.' And simple rules—keep your underwear on, don't hurt others, and help."

—*Marc Opperman, Austin, Texas*

"When we visit nearby sand dunes, my students talk about the wind which blows the sand, its speed in relation to the sand that it blows away. And when they sit on the dunes or walk, they discover the texture of sand, its weight and its impact on the human body. One child asked me, 'Miss Erum, I felt tired walking in the dunes. Why?' He realized that landscape matters. He experienced firsthand the connection of topography to the lives of humans. This is real learning which can never happen in the classroom."

—*Erum Kamran, Riyadh, Saudi Arabia*

Part 8

. . . .

The Nature-Rich Community

"A degraded habitat will produce degraded humans. If there is to be any true progress, then the entire life community must progress."

— THOMAS BERRY

"As humans we can not only make our ecological footprints as light as possible, but we can actually leave places better than when we came to them, making them places of delight."

— LOUISE CHAWLA,
COLLEGE OF ARCHITECTURE AND PLANNING,
UNIVERSITY OF COLORADO

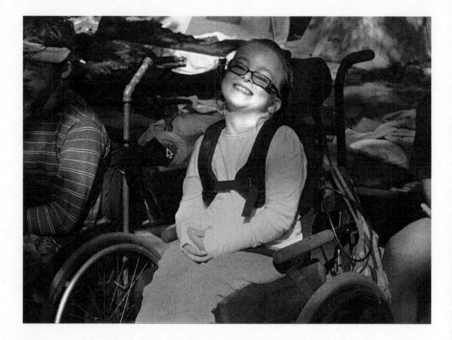

NOT BACK TO NATURE,
FORWARD TO NATURE

· ·

For centuries, people assumed that nature was in opposition to civilization. But, given the right circumstances, the reverse can be true. Nature can build community.

The term "social capital" refers to how well people look out for one another, and the sense of belonging and meaning that come with that.

When we consider the social capital of a community, why do we include only one species? Research suggests that when we interact with animals, the neurochemicals and hormones associated with social bonding are elevated. Encounters with other species can help children develop empathy. In fact, people who spend time in more natural environments in cities tend to nurture closer relationships with fellow human beings and to value community. And new studies indicate that the urban parks with the greatest biodiversity—the most species of other animals, in addition to humans—are also the parks that have the greatest beneficial effects on psychological health and well-being.

One reason for this, I believe, is that when we are in the presence of other animals, and aware of this at a deeper level, we do not feel alone. I've called this phenomenon "human/nature social capital." Simply put, we're part of a larger community.

Some research shows that, given the right conditions, greening neighborhoods may help reduce violence in the home and beyond. Natural playgrounds encourage more egalitarian and inclusive play. They may also reduce bullying and lead to more fantasy play—the kind that strengthens executive function, the ability to control oneself.

So if we want more-resilient and self-directed children, and kinder adults, one way to accomplish that is by not only prizing diversity in our cities, but biodiversity, too. As of 2008, for the first time in human history, more people now live in cities than in the countryside. That means one of two things: the gradual decay of the already-fragile relationship between humans and the rest of the natural world or the beginning of a nature-rich city.

On April 23, 2015, a prestigious international group of leading scientists—including a Nobel Prize winner and several nominees—issued the Helsinki Alert of Biodiversity and Health, affirming the necessity of nearby nature to human health and the need for a new approach to urban planning and policies. (The long list of signatories included a Nobel Prize winner, several nominees, and several researchers from the Karolinska Institute, who are responsible for awarding the Nobel Prize for Physiology and/or Medicine, among others.)

In the Alert, published in the *Annals of Medicine*, the scientists stated: "Urban living in built, asphalt-covered environments with little green space, together with the use of processed water and food, may not provide us with the broad microbial stimulation necessary for the development of a balanced immune function... Politicians and stakeholders in urban planning must become more aware about the effects of natural environments on human health ... People are not moving in masses back to the countryside, but elements of country life should be moved to cities."

We can transform our cities and communities into engines of biodiversity and human health. More than a sustainable (as in energy-efficient, survivable) future; we need a nature-rich future.

WHAT EVERY PARENT, TEACHER, AND YOUNG PERSON NEEDS TO KNOW ABOUT THE COMING OPPORTUNITIES IN NATURE-SMART CAREERS

Even as nature preschools, or forest schools as some are called in Europe, are growing in number, demand is outpacing supply.

Not long ago, I met some dedicated young women who were doing their student teaching at an impressive nature-based preschool. They made it clear that they'd love to pursue careers at similar schools, but they were discouraged about the prospects. Despite the growing demand from parents, the number of nature-based preschools still remains relatively low. "Is there a business school at your university?" I asked. They said there was.

"Have the business school and your education school ever considered working together to prepare future teachers to start your own preschools?" The students looked at one another. They had never heard of such a thing. Nor had the director of the preschool.

Why not? Probably because it doesn't exist. Bringing more nature experiences to education will be a challenging task, and teachers can't do it alone. Higher education, businesses, families, and the whole community must become involved. The good news is that the definition of green jobs is broadening beyond energy efficiency. New nature-smart careers are emerging. What if high schools and colleges helped students create a nature-rich future, and encouraged them to become outdoor entrepreneurs? There are some exciting careers that you—and your kids or students—may never have considered.

Here are nine suggested resources for you to help you begin to explore nature-smart careers with your kids: the Student Conservation Association, the National Outdoor Leadership School, USA Jobs, the Wilderness Medicine Institute, Leave No Trace Center for Outdoor Ethics, the Outdoor Industry Association, BackdoorJobs.com, REI

Outdoor School, and the Children & Nature Network's Natural Leaders Network.

For starters, consider these opportunities for jobs, careers, avocations, and entrepreneurial businesses:

Designer of biophilic homes and workplaces

Cutting-edge architects and industrial designers are including but moving beyond mere energy efficiency, as important as that is. Now they're designing products, homes, and workplaces that incorporate natural elements to improve health and productivity. Studies of workplaces created or retrofitted through biophilic design show improved product quality, customer satisfaction and innovation, and employee health. Learn about biophilic workplace design at HumanSpaces.com. Recommended book: *Biophilic Design: The Theory, Science, and Practice of Bringing Buildings to Life.* Video: *Biophilic Design: The Architecture of Life.* The Biomimicry Institute promotes learning from and emulating natural forms, processes, and ecosystems to create more sustainable and healthier human technologies and designs.

Nature-smart residential builder

They'll specialize in window-appeal (the view of nature from inside the home) — not just curb appeal. They'll know how to place a new house in sync with the sun's movements, use local materials to reflect the nature and history of the region, install a super-insulated green roof that can last eighty years, design for natural air-conditioning, and weave nature into homes and offices in even the most crowded urban neighborhoods. Here's one example of the communities of the future: Serenbe, a new town just outside Atlanta, Georgia, blends upscale energy-efficient housing with nature trails, vegetable gardens, rooftop gardens, and conservation.

🌿 Specialist in nature-smart employee benefits

Clif Bar headquarters in Emeryville, California, provides employees with on-site kayaks, paddles, and loaner bikes for local errands, and offers a rock-climbing wall. Companies have long used wilderness retreats as a reflective catalyst for leadership training. Now, to reduce employee stress and boost morale, companies such as Google, Yahoo, and *Sunset* magazine promote on-site organic vegetable gardens. At least one company offers weeklong nature camps for adults who need to recharge their physical, emotional, and intellectual batteries.

🌿 Nature-smart yard and garden specialist

This expert helps homeowners and businesses to reduce traditional lawns and replace them with bird-attracting native vegetation, butterfly gardens, chlorine-free natural swimming ponds, organic vegetable gardens, beehives, and places to raise chickens and ducks and gather eggs. As local governments continue to loosen regulations on yard farming, and as nearby production of food becomes more important, this specialty will become more popular.

🌿 Urban wildscaper

Urban designers, landscape architects, and other professionals who develop or redevelop neighborhoods that connect people to nature through the creation of biophilically designed buildings and preservation of natural land will be increasingly in demand. They will design and establish biodiverse parks, urban forests and community gardens, wildlife corridors, and other wild lands. Seattle recently announced plans for a massive urban forest that will include food producers. Wildscapers will also manage wildlife populations.

🌿 Outside-in decorator

These professionals will bring the outside in, creating or improving our homes to nurture health and well-being through nature: "living walls" of vegetation that purify air; indoor vertical vegetable gardens with automatic drip-irrigation systems; biophilic decorations such as twig furniture; lighting that adjusts throughout the day via light sensors at the windows; bird-warning elements for windows; indoor water gardens, and other living features. This goes way beyond feng shui.

🌿 New agrarian

Who's that? Urban farmers who design and operate community gardens. Designers and operators of vertical farms in high-rise buildings. Organic farmers and innovative vanguard ranchers who use sophisticated organic practices to produce food. The focus is on local, family-scale sustainable food, fiber, and fuel production in, near, and beyond cities. National Young Farmers Coalition is a farmer-led partnership focused on policy change, community, and online sharing of ideas and resources. The Greenhorns is a nonprofit that links up young farmers hungry for new ideas, yet who respect tradition.

🌿 Health-care provider who prescribes nature

As mentioned earlier, some pediatricians are now prescribing or recommending "green exercise" in parks and other natural settings to their young patients and their families. Hospitals, mental health centers, and nursing homes are creating healing gardens. The Portland, Oregon, parks department partners with physicians who send families to local parks, where park rangers serve as health para-professionals.

🌿 Nature therapist

Ecopsychologists and other wilderness therapy professionals are going mainstream. A few universities and colleges offer ecopsychology certificate programs, including Lewis & Clark College in

Portland, Oregon, and the Graduate Teacher Education Program at Mary Baldwin College in Staunton, Virginia. The American Psychological Association offers a short list of outdoor resources, from university programs to summer internships with wilderness therapy programs.

Green exercise trainer

Exercise appears to have better results if conducted outdoors, especially for psychological well-being. Green exercise trainers can help individuals and families individually or by organizing "green gyms" and family nature clubs. "People walkers" can help the elderly take a hike. Online primers: OutdoorFitness.com and MovNat.com. Recommended book: *Tina Vindum's Outdoor Fitness*.

Natural teacher

As parents and educators learn more about the brain-stimulating power of learning in natural settings, demand will increase for nature-based schools and nature-based experiential learning, providing new opportunities for natural teachers, natural playscape, and school-garden designers. Librarians can be natural teachers, too, creating bioregional Natural Libraries. Learn about nature-based preschools from GreenHeartsInc.org. Also see ChildrenandNature.org.

Bioregional guide

We'll see the emergence of the citizen naturalist who, as professionals or volunteers, help people get to know where they live. Through such organizations as Exploring a Sense of Place, guides help groups have a deeper understanding of the life surrounding them. Think of these guides as nature-smart Welcome Wagons who develop a deeper sense of personal and local identity.

How One Young Woman
Found Her Calling
in a Canyon

●●●●●●●●●●●●●●●●●●●●●●●●●●●●●●

E rin Lau, thirty-one, recalls how an early path through the canyon woods in San Diego led her to a creative career and calling.

"When I was young, the things that really captivated me were outdoor explorations, basic wilderness survival, and stories set in nature," she says. "I yearned to live in the countryside or the forest as a child, and made the best of what I could in our stucco suburbia." She recalls growing up in San Diego, "always building forts with my friends in the canyons that surrounded my house, trying out new building methods, being inspired by Native American huts and lifestyles that I would see on field trips or in books." Never mind that the neighborhood's community association would send people to tear down her tree houses. She rebuilt. And rebuilt.

Today, she's a landscape architect in Seattle. "My work is creating spaces in the built environment for natural life to flourish where it otherwise would not," she says. "Nature itself has inspired this work by its ability to regenerate, recycle and use what it already has. When I look back at my childhood, I realize that I didn't need fully wild natural surroundings to inspire me. I took what I had. Just the basics can do: trees, waterways, some insects and birds—imagination can do the rest. I'm grateful that my imagination was strong enough to fill in the blanks with a more idealized nature, back then, because now that's what I do every day as my job!"

THE ESSENTIAL ROLE OF LIBRARIES IN CREATING NATURE-RICH COMMUNITIES

The seeds of the future are planted in our homes and neighborhoods, but also in our businesses and in the institutions of our cities. Schools, museums, zoos, service organizations, churches, and more—these are the connectors of community.

Libraries (including school libraries), exist in every kind of neighborhood; they already serve as community hubs; they're often supported by Friends groups; they have existing resources (nature books); they're often more flexible than schools; they're known for being safe—and they're a perfect, if unexpected, institution to connect people to nature. As a parent, teacher, community—or, of course, librarian—you can build community support for turning a local and regional library into a Natural Library (or a nature-smart library, or Naturebrary, as some folks call a library that maximizes natural elements).

Here are some suggestions for what parents, conservation groups, librarians, and others can do to create Natural Libraries:

🍃 **Work with librarians to offer outdoor reading areas on library property.**
The Middle Country Public Library in Centereach, New York, created the Nature Explorium, converting an adjacent five-thousand-square-foot area into an outdoor learning environment, "including a climbing/crawling area, messy materials area, building area, nature art area, music and performance area, planting area, gathering/conversation place, reading area, and water feature," reports *American Libraries* magazine. Kids are watched by library staff, and every child is required to have a caregiver on the grounds. The Nature Explorium was immediately popular and even attracted some new donors.

🍃 Help libraries become information hubs for outdoor activities.

Parents, teachers, and kids can gather the information for the library. Offer area maps, pamphlets on local nature, brochures for hiking clubs, and registries for community gardens. Libraries can set up a nature connection kiosk offering free information about garden clubs, hiking clubs, and family nature club tool kits in multiple languages, and encourage the clubs to meet at the library. In Petawawa, Ontario (pop. 16,000), the Parks and Recreation Department and the Public Library are working together to offer free kayak and stand-up paddleboard rentals and lessons.

🍃 Offer outdoor gear for checkout by children and others.

Some libraries, like those in Petawawa, are already checking out such outdoor gear as fishing rods, snowshoes, GPS units (for outdoor geocache hunts for treasures hidden by library staff members across town). A library-based snowshoeing program is so popular that there's a waiting list. With the help of parents, schools, and local conservation organizations and outdoor recreation companies, libraries can assemble loanable daypacks containing binoculars, compasses, safety kits, guides to hiking trails and local flora and fauna, and other regional nature information. Local PTAs and PTSAs could help with volunteers and raising funds for this and other Natural Library offerings.

🍃 Think outside the library walls: Storytime Trails and Book Trees.

The Petawawa Library/Parks and Rec partnership also created a Storytime Trail. "Children start walking at the beginning of one of our trails, read the first page of a book with their parents, continue another 100 feet to find the second page and continue along the trail until they have read a good portion of the book," report Kelly Thompson and Colin Coyle, who represent the library and parks departments. "The Library side of the project promotes literacy while the Recreation side of walking to each page gets them active outdoors. We couldn't dream of a better match." They also have created "book trees." In our local playground, a cluster of five trees have been used in the design of a free outdoor library (the trees used were downed in a microburst). The concept is to "take a book, leave a book, and share a book."

🍃 **Build bioregional identity and regional biodiversity.**
Offer a special section in the library for these books, and Friends of the Library groups can stock the library book-nook stores with nature books, especially ones about the local region. Natural Libraries can provide a meeting place for people who want to explore and discuss the nature of their own region. They can organize lectures and convene groups of architects, urban designers, educators, physicians, birders, and many others to plan the re-naturing of the surrounding community. Natural Libraries can also help create neighborhood butterfly zones—or a national homegrown park—beginning on the library's own grounds. They can increase backyard biodiversity by partnering with natural history museums and botanical gardens. For example, libraries could hand out free packets of seeds to families who want to help bring back butterfly and bird migration routes.

🍃 **Help libraries build new partnerships with nature-focused and family-oriented organizations, and diverse cultural groups.**
A library is a perfect place to convene parks departments, conservation groups, natural history museums, schools, botanical gardens (especially horticultural libraries), and local businesses (particularly from the outdoor industry) to plant the seeds of environmental literacy. In turn, these organizations can promote the library, and grow local support for the library's financial needs. The Sun Ray library in St. Paul, Minnesota, currently conducts family reading hours in Hmong, Spanish, Somali, and English, and hopes to draw on the rich nature traditions in those communities.

Libraries can also convene family nature clubs: multiple families that band together to organize nature outings. Also, by encouraging the growth of family nature clubs, Natural Libraries will not only help families get outside, but will be building a widening constituency to support libraries generally.

🍃 Use tech to expand the constituency for libraries, parks, and nature.

Antje Dun, chief librarian for the Australian Conservation Foundation, offers these suggestions: spread the word through a Pinterest page or Twitter hashtag devoted to natured libraries; set up a website; build a community of natured librarians using Facebook; create an online newsletter with project topics for natured libraries, such as seed banks, promoting your bioregional identity, nature backpacks, outdoor reading spaces; create a YouTube channel, and ask librarians and library users to make and post videos about natured libraries and their activities.

🍃 Design or remodel libraries with nature in mind.

The Sun Ray Natural Library Project's renovation project includes natural elements throughout, including green spaces inside and in an adjacent park, an outdoor reading garden, wildlife-friendly plants, rain gardens, and dozens of newly planted trees. There's also a children's "Nature Nook" inside the library with interactive wildlife features and doors to the children's outdoor reading garden. There will be a public art installation there called "House Trees" where little houses will be placed up in the air on artistically rendered tree branches.

🍃 Parents and other community members can work for nature-smart libraries through a Friends of the Library group.

Support your local Natural Librarian. If you're not already a member of a Friends of the Library group, join and build community support for bringing more nature into the library and more library services into nature. If there isn't a Friends of the Library organization attached to your local library, create one—and start a Nature Library committee. Learn more about Friends groups at the United for Libraries website.

🌿 **Lend your support to nature-smart librarians across the country.**

Reaching beyond localities, we need national or international campaigns to bring together librarians, publishers, parents, and other stakeholders to devise a campaign to naturalize libraries across the country and around the world. As Cicero said, "If you have a garden and a library, you have everything." Or almost.

VITAMIN N FOR THE SOUL: THE POTENTIAL OF FAITH-BASED ORGANIZATIONS

One of my sons once asked me if a connection to a higher power is, in fact, an underutilized sense—one that some people find activated in nature. This is the same son who, when he was five, asked, "Are God and Mother Nature married, or just good friends?" Great questions.

I shared those thoughts in *The Nature Principle* and *Last Child in the Woods*. Since the publication of those books, I've been surprised and impressed by the support that many religious leaders of all faiths, and nonbelievers as well, have offered to the movement to connect people to the natural world. I've come to believe that smart spiritual people intuitively understand that all spiritual life begins with a sense of wonder, and that sense is usually formed early in childhood, often in natural settings.

Most religious traditions, especially in indigenous cultures, intimate or actively offer ways to discover the divine in the natural world.

Which leads us to the next point: Faith-based communities and religious organizations could play a much larger role in helping children and adults know the world, and beyond, through nature.

Here are a few of the ways that places of worship can reduce nature-deficit disorder and make gentler the life of the world:

- In sermons and in practice, religious leaders can explore the spiritual value of connecting children to nature. GreenFaith offers curricula and other resources for Christian, Jewish, Islamic, Hindu, and Buddhist teachings on the environment. Consider mindfulness (rooted in Buddhism, but not restricted to it) toward creation, including human beings.

- Religious organizations, already major sponsors of early childhood education, can dramatically increase the availability of nature-based preschools and childcare centers. Green Hearts is a good source of information on nature-based early childhood education, including its guide *25 Easy Nature Play Ideas for Early Childhood Centers.*

- Support your local nature camp. Church camps and nature retreats have a long tradition of connecting kids to nature, but many have been eliminated or reduced in recent years by budget cuts and land sales. Place more emphasis on the nature connection at existing camps, and create new ones, including interfaith camps for children of all backgrounds and spiritual traditions. The American Camp Association offers tips and information on how to preserve or create new ones.

- Places of worship can promote family nature clubs and organize other outdoor activities for families. Nationally, the Christian Hiking Network and the Muslim Outdoor Camping and Hiking Association organize such outings. They also connect people within and among neighborhoods by forming nature networks.

● On their grounds or other properties, faith-based centers can adapt some of the tools and techniques of the green schoolyards move- ment (see C&NN's Green Schoolyards for Health Communities Project) and help transform the landscapes and waters of their own communities. Reach beyond the grounds. Encourage families to transform their yards and neighborhoods into places welcoming to native species.

● Many religious leaders believe it's time to move beyond the divi- sion in biblical interpretation between the words dominion and stewardship. They say: Of course we have dominion; look what we're doing to the Earth—but why would we want to trash God's creation? Many congregations, conservative and liberal, now in- volve children, families, and individuals in conservation working locally and globally. The Blessed Tomorrow coalition, launched in 2014 by ecoAmerica's MomentUs initiative, brings together representatives from a broad range of faith traditions to work on climate change. Congregations are invited to sign a commitment "to walk more gently on the earth and to inspire others to lead on climate in their homes, places of worship, and communities." Even if not everyone agrees on the particulars, all can join together to heal our home.

● Places of worship can take a leading role in advocating for the hu- man right of all children to connect to nature, regardless of ethnic- ity, race, sexual orientation, economic level, abilities or disabilities, or religion. The list of the benefits of time spent in nature include better physical and mental health and enhanced cognitive abilities. To that list we can add the life of the spirit. All children, not just a few, deserve the natural gifts of the creation.

Belonging

....

In so many of our communities, fear remains one of the great barriers between people and the natural world. Even so, the new nature movement is fueled by hope, and by the knowledge that life needs life, and life is good.

Sarah Walker, a recent college graduate who lives in Kingston, Ontario, helped create the Child and Nature Alliance of Canada. She recently wrote about her special place in nature near her home, from which a nature-rich future is visible:

"I am sitting on a hill overlooking a wooded forest that defines the landscape of my favorite place in the whole world. I lie with my back against a snowdrift and my snowshoes strapped to my feet." As she gazed up into the cloudless sky, she found herself trying to put a name to what she was feeling. "Today, for the first time, I can tell you with one word why I fell in love with the children and nature movement. It is also the same reason I sit outside in this frigid weather: *security*.

"As I sit atop this hill, I'm about to finish school in the next couple of months and I'm not really sure what my next step will be. In spite of this, I know that no matter what life brings my way, I can sit in this spot and watch the sun rise and set below this tree line."

MAKE YOUR CITY THE BEST IN THE NATION (OR THE WORLD) FOR CONNECTING FAMILIES TO NATURE

One key measurement of our future will be whether cities are healthy places for children and nature. A city that accomplishes that goal is one that's good, or, at least, better for everyone of every age, with or without kids of their own.

When Miranda Andersen was thirteen, she sent me a description of the nature-rich future she hopes to help create. "I can almost picture houses in the future built only out of windows. A place where parking lots are turned back into natural wilderness or made into green spaces or at least having green spaces inside of them," she wrote. "Schools where you learn outside and with the roofs that are gardens and with rainwater collected to flush toilets. Places where people can grow their own food. A place where happiness is more important than money. Where everyone has some access to some kind of nature. How about creating a way of life that turns endangered plants or animals into a never-ending supply? Then maybe there would be hope instead of despair."

Through a TEDx talk and a film she made about nature-deficit disorder, Miranda, who lives near Vancouver, B.C., is already helping build that future.

So here's a challenge. What can each of us do to help make our communities nature-rich? Can your city become the nation's (or the world's) Best City for Children and Nature? Leaders who decide to make that idea part of their region's DNA could establish two-to-five-year plans with benchmarks and reachable goals. National or international benchmarks don't yet exist (though those measures may be in place by the time you read this, through an effort by the National League of Cities). Here's a starter list of suggested goals to aim for:

Build a vision.

Reconnecting today's children and families to nature is an issue that brings people together across political, religious, and economic barriers like no other. Usually, cities work through envisioning groups that focus primarily on economic competition (for instance, "Our new Silicon Valley is going to be bigger than your Silicon Valley"). But what if your city were to reimagine its future by looking through the prism of *nature*? What would its health care and public health systems, its education system, its residential developments and redevelopments and shopping areas be like?

What about its economic health; its ability to market itself to the most creative people and businesses from around the world? What, then, would the future look like?

🍃 Launch a community campaign to Leave No Child Inside.

Encourage parents, grandparents, public health workers, and others to help organize your community to confront the pandemics of inactivity and nature-deficit disorder and promote outdoor exercise. Get involved with or help start a community, regional, state, or provincial campaign. More than 120 already exist in North America; these groups are your nearby allies. See ChildrenandNature.org to learn about existing campaigns and how to start a new one.

🍃 Promote nature-smart schools.

With support of local businesses, launch a Nature-Smart Campaign for education: partner with schools, PTAs, or other groups to create regional Natural Teacher awards or fellowships, honoring the teachers who insist on getting their students outside to learn. Is there a positive impact of nature-rich education on student testing? Do students and the public know about the wildlife of their own bioregion? Perhaps a business could sponsor a citywide or statewide children's essay contest on how they connect with nature.

🍃 Engage health providers.

Increase the number of pediatricians and other health professionals prescribing nature. Start a Natural Health campaign. For example, hospitals, physicians, parks, botanical gardens, and businesses can work together to raise awareness about the health benefits of nature experiences, with a special focus on the neighborhoods with the least amount of natural habitat; they can then build a system to measure the impact of your programs on obesity and health-care costs. Mary Jo Kreitzer, a nursing professor at the University of Minnesota and director of the university's Center for

Spirituality and Healing, believes that her city and state should set a goal of becoming the healthiest state in the country, and that viewing the future through the prism of nature could help Minnesota reach that goal.

🍃 Galvanize businesses.

Challenge businesses to build a nature-rich economy and market the region as a great place for children and nature. Measure the region's progress by increases in local nature-based tourism, rising property values adjacent to new parks, new jobs created, and businesses attracting people looking for a better quality of life, better schools, and a healthier workforce.

🍃 Expand natural space, biodiversity, and local food production.

Work to increase your city's nature trails, bike paths, natural parkland, and wildlife corridors. Increase the number of land trusts in your urban region by engaging national organizations such as the Nature Conservancy or the Trust for Public Land (which focuses mainly on preserving native habitat in urban areas) or smaller regional ones like the San Dieguito River Valley Conservancy, which is creating an ocean-to-mountains trail in San Diego. Also, support policies that keep farming families on their land, strengthen land trust law, and decrease property owners' liability when they allow children to play on open land.

🍃 Create wildlife and childlife corridors on private land.

Botanical gardens in each city can help create a De-Central Park by declaring that all the green spots of a city, from pocket parks to community gardens to green roofs, be viewed as one great park or wildlife corridor. Botanical gardens, zoos, aquaria, and other institutions can declare an ambitious ten-year goal, the creation of a vast network of wildlife corridors established by ordinary citizens, yard to yard, city to city—a Homegrown National Park, or, better yet, a Worldwide Homegrown Park. Make sure ordinances and legislation encourages backyard gardens, community gardens, and organic farms.

🌿 Help truly green your cityscape.

Push for better urban planning and in developing and redeveloping areas, including tree-planting guidelines, more natural parks, and walkable neighborhoods. Lobby for affordable public transportation, so that urban children and families can easily reach nature areas. The Rails to Trails Conservancy supports former rail lines that have been converted to multi-use trails, for transportation as well as recreation. Urge developers and builders to create green communities, or, better yet, renovate decaying neighborhoods and shopping malls with green oases—urban ecovillages, button parks, and other natural park spaces—that connect children and adults to nature.

🌿 Protect open space and reduce nature-deficit disorder.

Developers often leave set-aside land—slices of property not large enough to be playing fields, not located conveniently to be pocket parks, but that can serve as islands of wildness that are great for kids' imaginative play. These and other urban and suburban plots can be transformed into adventure playgrounds or "wild zones" that provide kids with a supervised (by an adult, at a distance) vacant lot filled with old tires, boards, tools—and places to build and dig. Pledge to dedicate a portion of any proposed open space to children and families in the surrounding area, with, ideally, nature centers to provide education for schools and outdoor-oriented preschools. Download the "Health Benefits of Parks" report by the Trust for Public Land.

🌿 Reduce fear of the outdoors.

Enlist media to increase awareness of comparative risks (the risk of child obesity compared to the risk of playing outdoors). Reduce real dangers in some neighborhoods, including traffic and toxins. Is the legal profession involved? In an overly litigious society, families, schools, and communities play it safe, creating "risk-free" environments that create greater risks later. In your neighborhood, challenge conventional covenants and restrictions that discourage or prohibit natural play. Rewrite the rules to allow kids to build forts and tree houses and to plant gardens. Make sure they have access to nearby nature.

🍃 Encourage young people to build community through service organizations.

Boy Scouts, Girl Scouts, Camp Fire U.S.A., and 4-H have changed with the times, but remain dedicated to connecting children to nature. Investigate family nature programs sponsored by conservation groups such as the Sierra Club Student Coalition. Consider the many opportunities that are offered for children and teenagers by public park systems, including junior ranger and junior naturalist programs. "Most ranger programs have ranger ride-alongs, and other formal and informal programs to engage the interest of teens," according to Rich Dolesh, a director of public policy at the National Recreation and Park Association. Older youths can join the National Park Service's Youth Conservation Corps, an eight-to-ten-week summer work and experience program. And they can get community leadership training, focused on connecting future generations of children to the natural world through the Natural Leaders Network.

🍃 Establish a Human/Nature Report Card.

Sponsored by public and private agencies, a regional Human/Nature Report Card would include but go beyond traditional measures of profit and revenue from outdoor recreation (fishing, boating, hiking, and so on), or concerns about the negative results of environmental toxins; it would consider the positive economic impact on public mental and physical health, education, and jobs.

Measures of the influence of the natural world on child and adult obesity and depression, for example, could be translated into direct and indirect costs of health care and lost productivity. The positive impact of parks, open space, and nearby nature (which we know more about) on property values could also be measured and reported. The economic benefits of outdoor classrooms and place-based education might be estimated. We also could see the creation of many jobs, both traditional and new, if we widen the definition of "green jobs" to include employment or entrepreneurial companies that connect people to nature. Such an ongoing, comprehensive regional human/nature study—linking human health and economic well-being to the health of the bioregion—would give support to policymakers who pursue the goal of connecting our families and future generations to the natural world.

Give your city the Best City for Children and Nature Award.

Say your city or state sets these or similar goals, measures progress toward them, and then, in two to five years it reaches them. Celebrate. Declare your community the Best City in the Nation (or World) for Children and Nature. Broadcast this, market this, be proud of it. And if a mayor of another city wants to argue that his or her city is better for children and nature than yours, well, that's great. If cities can compete symbolically through football teams, why not compete in reality to reach this goal line?

Other Voices

"This is a win for an elected official. For mayors, the power to convene is the most important power we have to bring a city together for children and nature."

— Salt Lake City Mayor Ralph Becker,
president of the National League of Cities

"In cities like Rio de Janeiro, the rich and poor meet on the beach, crossing the giant social abyss that separates them . . . All we need to do is open the doors and take that first step with children. Nature does the rest, and truth be told, it does it well."

—Daniela Benavides, Rio de Janeiro, Brazil

"I love nature because I love people. I would do all I could to share with my community the joy of nature."

—Juan Martinez, on growing up in South Central L.A.

PEACE LIKE A RIVER

. . . .

Beyond our homes and cities and nations, a great river flows through a larger community. It moves inexorably toward this conclusion: All children need nature, not only those whose parents appreciate nature, not only those of a certain economic class or culture or set of abilities. All children, and future generations, have a right to a nature-rich future, and the option to share in the responsibilities that come with that right.

In September 2012, the World Congress of the International Union for Conservation of Nature (IUCN)—attended by more than ten thousand people representing the governments of 150 nations and more than one thousand nongovernmental organizations—met in Jeju, South Korea. There, the IUCN passed a resolution, "the Child's Right to Connect with Nature and to a Healthy Environment." That resolution recognizes "concern about the increasing disconnection of people and especially children from nature, and the adverse consequences for both healthy child development ('nature-deficit disorder') as well as responsible stewardship for nature and the environment in the future."

And it recognizes that "children, since they are an inalienable part of nature, not only have the right to a healthy environment, but also to a connection with nature and to the gifts of nature for their physical and psychological health and ability to learn and create." In a world in which so much divides us, the river of that idea moves us together. And in that river is a sense of peace.

If, in solitude or with the help of a special adult or friend, a child finds a special place in nature, it can offer solace and more in decades to come. A psychiatrist who works with children with the symptoms of ADHD told me how he sometimes slides into mild depressions. He grew up in Michigan, and spent countless hours along streams, in the woods, crossing fields of wildflowers. "And that was how I found peace as a child," he said. "So, when I begin to feel depressed, I use self-hypnosis to go there again, to call up those memories." He calls them "meadow memories."

In these difficult times, such talk of meadow memories of wild things may seem beside the point. Or frivolous. Erring on the side of fear seems to make more sense. Yet ongoing research suggests just how restorative those memories can be, how vital they are to a child's or an adult's resilience.

The violence of nature itself is a fact, but this is also true: by assaulting nature, we raise the odds that we will assault one another. By bringing nature into our lives, we invite humility. By creating meaningful connections between people and nature, we can potentially reduce human violence in our world.

We've seen how experiences in nature can build a sense of community, and can help bring families and friends closer together, in loving ways, and can bring to us a sense of shared meaning that transcends our differences.

There's a time for hypervigilance, and there's a time to pay a different kind of attention. In a recent op-ed, Larry Rosen, MD, a champion of the children and nature movement, shared this definition of mindfulness from *The Three Questions*, a children's book based on a story by Leo Tolstoy: "Realize that the most important time is now, the most important person is the one you're with and the most important thing to do is what you are doing right here, right now . . . that you will never make all the stress in the world disappear . . . Take time to look someone in the eyes, listen to her story, and let her know that you hear her. Be willing to sit in the mud until it settles and the water clears."

The path along the river and through the woods is no panacea. But our kids deserve a break. So do we. To create meadow memories that can last a lifetime, we can start by taking our children and grandchildren on a hike. We can enrich our homes with native species, plant school gardens, rethink the environments of our neighborhoods, prescribe nature, and much more.

We can create a richer, more peaceful life and, as the years go by, return to that special place in the heart where wonder grows.

ACKNOWLEDGMENTS

I am deeply appreciative of the work of many other writers in this field. In addition to the original material provided in these pages, *Vitamin N* cites good books, websites, and organizations. These sources are listed in the text or as recommended resources at the end of the book.

My gratitude to the many people who support the organizations and individuals working to reconnect people and the natural world.

Special thanks to the staff, volunteers, and board of directors of the Children & Nature Network, and to those educators, health professionals, and others who have lent their expertise to these pages. Among them, Cheryl Charles, Joseph Baust, Tamra Willis, Herb Broda, Clifford Knapp, and Robin Moore.

Thanks, too, to my editor, Amy Gash, and publisher, Elisabeth Scharlett, and the other great folks at Algonquin Books; and to Jim Levine, Jackie Green, Robyn Bjornsson, and Suz Lipman, and to Matthew Louv who helped mightily with the research; to my wife, Kathy, and older son, Jason, who always offer moral support and insight; to Peter Kaye, who passed during the week that this project came to a conclusion, and to my longtime friend and editor, Dean Stahl, who has stuck by me through all my recent books, both thick and thin.

Bibliography and Recommended Reading

Note: For a more complete list of excellent books and other resources, see RichardLouv.com.

Acclimatizing, Steve Van Matre (Amer. Camping Assn., 1972).

In Accord with Nature: Helping Students Form an Environmental Ethic Using Outdoor Experience and Reflection, Clifford E. Knapp (Eric Clearinghouse on Rural, 1998).

The Art of Mountain Biking: Singletrack Skills for All Riders, Robert Hurst (Globe Pequot Press, 2011).

Asphalt to Ecosystems: Design Ideas for Schoolyard Transformation, Sharon Gamson Danks (New Village Press, 2010).

Attracting Birds, Butterflies and Other Backyard Wildlife, David Mizejewski (Creative Homeowner, 2004).

Backyard Bees, Douglas Purdie (Murdoch Books, 2015).

Backyard Bird Watching for Kids: How to Attract, Feed, and Provide Homes for Birds, George H. Harrison (Willow Creek Press, 1997).

Backyard Livestock: Raising Good, Natural Food for Your Family, George B. Looby (Countryman Press, 2007).

Balcony Gardening: A Beginners Guide to Starting a Beautiful Balcony Garden, Stuart Cooper (Kindle Edition).

Basic Canoeing: All the Skills and Tools You Need to Get Started, Jon Rounds, ed. (Stackpole Books, 2003).

Bay Area Wild: A Celebration of the Natural Heritage of the San Francisco Bay Area, Galen A. Rowell (Sierra Club Books, 1997).

Be in a Treehouse, Pete Nelson (Harry N. Abrams, 2014).

Beyond Ecophobia: Reclaiming the Heart in Nature Education, David Sobel (Orion Society, 1999).

Big Tracks, Little Tracks: Following Animal Prints, Millicent E. Selsam (HarperCollins, 1998).

Biophilia, Edward O. Wilson (Harvard University Press, 1986).

Biophilic Design: The Theory, Science, and Practice of Bringing Buildings to Life, Stephen R. Kellert, Judith Heerwagen, and Martin Mador (Wiley, 2008).

Birthright: People and Nature in the Modern World, Stephen Kellert (Yale University Press, 2014).

The Book of Gardening Projects for Kids: 101 Ways to Get Kids Outside, Dirty, and Having Fun, Whitney Cohen and John Fisher (Timber Press, 2012).

Bringing Nature Home: How You Can Sustain Wildlife with Native Plants, Douglas W. Tallamy (Timber Press, 2007).

The Bumper Book of Nature: A User's Guide to the Great Outdoors, Stephen Moss (Crown, 2010).

Cabins: A Guide to Building Your Own Nature Retreat, David Stiles and Jeanie Stiles (Firefly Books, 2001).

Camp Out!: The Ultimate Kids' Guide, Lynn Brunelle (Workman, 2007).

Career Ideas for Kids Who Like Animals and Nature, Diane Lindsey Reeves (Checkmark Books, 2007).

Catch a Fish, Throw a Ball, Fly a Kite (Three Rivers Press, 2004).

Childhood and Nature: Design Principles for Educators, David Sobel (Stenhouse Publishers, 2008).

Children's Special Places, David Sobel (Wayne State University Press, 2001).

A Child's Garden: Enchanting Outdoor Spaces for Children and Parents, Molly Dannenmaier (Simon & Schuster, 1998).

A Child's Introduction to the Night Sky: The Story of the Stars, Planets, and Constellations—and How You Can Find Them in the Sky, Michael Driscoll and Meredith Hamilton (Black Dog & Leventhal Publishers, 2004).

Climbing Back, Mark Wellman and John Flinn (WRS Group, 1992).

The Cloudspotter's Guide: The Science, History, and Culture of Clouds, Gavin Pretor-Pinney (Perigee, 2007).

Community Gardens: Grow Your Own Vegetables and Herbs, Susan Burns Chong (Rosen Pub Group, 2014).

Compact Cabins: Simple Living in 1000 Square Feet or Less, Gerald Rowan (Storey Books, 2010).

The Complete Book of Kites and Kite Flying, Will H. Yolen (Simon & Schuster, 1976).

The Complete Compost Gardening Guide: Banner batches, grow heaps, comforter compost, and other amazing techniques for saving time and money, and producing the most flavorful, nutritious vegetables ever, Deborah L. Martin and Barbara Pleasant (Storey Publishing, 2008).

The Complete Mushroom Hunter: An Illustrated Guide to Finding, Harvesting, and Enjoying Wild Mushrooms, Gary Lincoff (Quarry Books, 2010).

Cooked: A Natural History of Transformation, Michael Pollan (Penguin Books, 2014).

A Country Called Childhood: Children and the Exuberant World, Jay Griffiths (Counterpoint, 2014).

Coyote's Guide to Connecting with Nature, Jon Young, Ellen Haas, and Evan McGown (OWLlink Media, 2008).

Curious Critters, David FitzSimmons (Wild Iris Publishing, 2014).

The Curious Garden, Peter Brown (Little, Brown Books for Young Readers, 2009).

The Dangerous Book for Boys, Conn Iggulden and Hal Iggulden (William Morrow, 2012).

Diary of a Citizen-Scientist: Chasing Tiger Beetles and Other New Ways of Engaging the World, Sharman Apt Russell (Oregon State University Press, 2014).

Dirty Teaching: A Beginner's Guide to Learning Outdoors, Juliet Robertson (Independent Thinking Press, 2014).

Discovering Nature with Young Children: Part of the Young Scientist Series, Ingrid Chalufour and Karen Worth (Redleaf Press, 2003).

The Down and Dirty Guide to Camping with Kids: How to Plan Memorable Family Adventures and Connect Kids to Nature, Helen Olsson (Roost Books, 2012).

Drawn to Nature: Through the Journals of Clare Walker Leslie, Clare Walker Leslie (Storey Publishing, 2005).

Early Childhood Activities for a Greener Earth, Patty Born Selly (Redleaf Press, 2012).

Earth in Mind: On Education, Environment, and the Human Prospect, David W. Orr (Island Press, 2004).

The Ecology of Imagination in Childhood, Edith Cobb (Spring, 1998).

Ecopsychology: Science, Totems, and the Technological Species, Patricia Hasbach and Peter H. Kahn, Jr., eds. (The MIT Press, 2012).

Ecotherapy: Healing with Nature in Mind, Linda Buzzell and Craig Chalquist (Sierra Club Books, 2009).

The Edible Balcony: Growing Fresh Produce in Small Spaces, Alex Mitchell (Rodale Books, 2012).

Exploring a Sense of Place, How to create your own local program for reconnecting with Nature, Karen Harwell and Joanna Reynolds (Conexions, 2006).

Fed Up with Frenzy: Slow Parenting in a Fast-Moving World, Susan Sachs Lipman (Sourcebooks, 2012).

Feminine, Firm and Fit: Building a Strong, Lean Body, Kelli Calabrese and Debbie Hickey (Great Atlantic Publishing Group, 2004).

A Field Guide to Western Reptiles and Amphibians, Robert C. Stebbins (Houghton Mifflin Harcourt, 2003).

Finding Your Way Without Map or Compass, Harold Gatty (Dover Publications, 1999).

Foxfire Books, Eliot Wigginton and George P. Reynolds (Anchor Books Random House, 2011).

Get Out!: Outdoor Activities Kids Can Enjoy Anywhere (Except Indoors), Hallie Warshaw and Julie Brown (Sterling, 2003).

Get Outside Guide, Nancy Honovich and Julie Beer (National Geographic Children's Books, 2014).

Gone Fishin' with Kids: How to Take Your Kid Fishing and Still Be Friends, Joe Perrone and Manny Luftglass (Gone Fishin Enterprises, 1997).

Go Outside: Over 130 Activities for Outside Adventures, Nancy Blakey (Tricycle Press, 2002).

The Great Animal Orchestra: Finding the Origins of Music in the World's Wild Places, Bernie Krause (Back Bay Books, 2013).

The Great Work: Our Way into the Future, Thomas Berry (Bell Tower, 1999).

The Green Hour: A Daily Dose of Nature for Happier, Healthier, Smarter Kids, Todd Christopher (Roost Books, 2010).

Green Urbanism: Learning from European Cities, Timothy Beatley (Island Press, 2000).

Healing Gardens: Therapeutic Benefits and Design Recommendations, Clare Cooper Marcus and Marni Barnes, eds. (Wiley, 1999).

Healing Spaces: The Science of Place and Well-Being, Esther M. Sternberg (Belknap Press, 2010).

Home Grown: Adventures in Parenting off the Beaten Path, Ben Hewitt (Roost Books, 2014).

How to Build an Igloo: And Other Snow Shelters, Norbert E. Yankielun (W. W. Norton, 2007).

How to Raise a Wild Child: The Art and Science of Falling in Love with Nature, Scott D. Sampson (Houghton Mifflin Harcourt, 2015).

How to Rock Climb!, John Long (Falcon Guides, 2010).

The Human Age: The World Shaped by Us, Diane Ackerman (W. W. Norton & Company, 2014).

I Love Dirt!, Jennifer Ward, (Trumpeter, 2008).

I Love My World, Chris Holland (Wholeland Publications, 2012).

The Insect Book: A Basic Guide to the Collection and Care of Common Insects for Young Children, Connie Zakowski (Rainbow Books, 1996).

Joy of Hiking: Hiking the Trailmaster Way, John McKinney (Wilderness Press, 2005).

Julie of the Wolves, Jean Craighead George and John Schoenherr (HarperCollins, 2003).

The Jungle Book, Rudyard Kipling (Dover Publications, 2000).

Kaufman Field Guide to Insects of North America, Eric R. Eaton and Kenn Kaufman (Houghton Mifflin Harcourt, 2007).

Kayaking Made Easy: A Manual for Beginners with Tips for the Experienced, Dennis Stuhaug (Falcon Guides, 2013).

Keepers of the Animals: Native American Stories and Wildlife Activities for Children, Michael J. Caduto and Joseph Bruchac (Fulcrum Publishing, 1997).

Keeping a Nature Journal: Discover a Whole New Way of Seeing the World Around You, Clare Walker Leslie and Charles E. Roth (Storey, 2003).

Ken Libbrecht's Field Guide to Snowflakes, Kenneth Libbrecht (Voyageur Press, 2006).

The Kids' Book of Weather Forecasting: Build a Weather Station, "Read" the Sky & Make Predictions!, Mark Breen, Kathleen Friestad, and Michael Kline (Williamson Publishing, 2000).

Kids' Garden: 40 Fun Indoor and Outdoor Activities and Games, Whitney Cohen (Barefoot Books, 2010).

The Kids' Outdoor Adventure Book: 448 Great Things to Do in Nature Before You Grow Up, Stacy Tornio and Ken Keffer, Illustrations by Rachel Riordan (Falcon Guides, 2013).

Last Child in the Woods, Richard Louv (Algonquin, 2008).

Learning with Nature Idea Book: Creating Nurturing Outdoor Spaces for Children, Dimensions Educational Research Foundation, Nancy Rosenow, James R. Wike, and Valerie Cuppens (Arbor Day Foundation, 2007).

Let's Go Outside!: Outdoor Activities and Projects to Get You and Your Kids Closer to Nature, Jennifer Ward (Roost Books, 2009).

Living Lights: Fireflies in Your Backyard, Nancy Loewen (Picture Window Books, 2003).

The Lost Art of Finding Our Way, John Edward Huth (Belknap Press, 2013).

Making Healthy Places: Designing and Building for Health, Well-being, and Sustainability, Andrew L. Dannenberg, Howard Frumkin, and Richard J. Jackson (Island Press, 2011).

Making Outdoor Programs Accessible, Kathy Ambrosini (Mohonk Preserve, 2005) (also available online http://www.recpro.org /assets/Library/Accessibility/mohonk_nature_access_manual.pdf).

Mammal Tracks & Sign: A Guide to North American Species, Mark Elbroch (Stackpole Books, 2003).

Mental Health, Naturally: The Family Guide to Holistic Care for a Healthy Mind and Body, Kathi J. Kemper (American Academy of Pediatrics, 2010).

Moving the Classroom Outdoors: Schoolyard-Enhanced Learning in Action, Herbert W. Broda (Stenhouse Publishers, 2011).

My Nature Journal, Adrienne Olmstead (Pajaro, 1999).

National Geographic Kids Everything Weather: Facts, Photos, and Fun That Will Blow You Away, Kathy Furgang (National Geographic Children's Books, 2012).

Natural Learning: The Life History of an Environmental Schoolyard, Robin C. Moore and Herb H. Wong (Mig Communications, 1997).

The Natural Remedy Bible, John Lust and Michael Tierra (Gallery Books, 2008).

A Natural Sense of Wonder: Connecting Kids with Nature through the Seasons, Rick Van Noy (University of Georgia Press, 2008).

The Nature Connection: An Outdoor Workbook for Kids, Families, and Classrooms, Clare Walker Leslie (Storey Publishing, 2010).

The Nature Principle, Richard Louv (Algonquin, 2011).

Nature Seeker Workbook, Lawrence Wade (n/a, 2013).

Nature's Notes: Bite-Sized Learning & Projects for All Ages, Judy Burris and Wayne Richards (Willow Creek Books, 2012).

New Treehouses of the World, Pete Nelson (Harry N. Abrams, 2009).

The Omnivore's Dilemma: A Natural History of Four Meals, Michael Pollan (Penguin, 2007).

The Organic Lawn Care Manual: A Natural, Low-Maintenance System for a Beautiful, Safe Lawn, Paul Tukey (Storey Publishing, 2007).

The Outdoor Athlete, Courtenay Schurman and Doug Schurman (Human Kinetics, 2008).

Pilates for the Outdoor Athlete, Lauri Stricker (Fulcrum Publishing, 2007).

Place-Based Education: Connecting Classrooms and Communities, David Sobel (Orion Society, 2005).

Planting a Rainbow, Lois Ehlert (HMH Books for Young Readers, 1988).

Rewilding Our Hearts: Building Pathways of Compassion and Coexistence, Marc Bekoff (New World Library, 2014).

The Rodale Book of Composting: Easy Methods for Every Gardener, Grace Gershuny and Deborah L. Martin, eds. (Rodale Books, 1992).

Rooted in the Earth: Reclaiming the African American Environmental Heritage, Dianne D. Glave (Chicago Review Press, 2010).

Roots, Shoots, Buckets & Boots: Gardening Together with Children, Sharon Lovejoy (Workman, 1999).

A Sand County Almanac, Aldo Leopold (Ballantine Books, 1986).

Scraping Heaven: A Family's Journey Along the Continental Divide, Cindy Ross (International Marine/Ragged Mountain Press, 2002).

The Secret Life of a Snowflake: An Up-Close Look at the Art and Science of Snowflakes, Kenneth Libbrecht (Voyageur Press, 2010).

The Sense of Wonder, Rachel Carson (HarperCollins, 1998).

The Sextant Handbook, Bruce Bauer (International Marine/Ragged Mountain Press, 1995).

Sharing Nature with Children, Joseph Cornell (Dawn Publications, 1998).

Shelters, Shacks & Shanties: The Classic Guide to Building Wilderness Shelters, D. C. Beard (Dover, 2004).

Smart Moves: Why Learning Is Not All in Your Head, Carla Hannaford (Great River Books, 2007).

Smithsonian's Everything You Need to Know About Snakes (DK Children, 2013).

Snakes! A Kid's Book of Cool Images and Amazing Facts About Snakes, John Yost (CreateSpace Independent Publishing Platform, 2013).

Snakes: The Evolution of Mystery in Nature, Harry W. Greene (University of California Press, 2000).

The Stick Book, Fiona Danks and Jo Schofield (Frances Lincoln, 2012).

Sunflower Houses: Inspiration from the Garden, Sharon Lovejoy (Workman, 2001).

Surfer's Start-Up: A Beginner's Guide to Surfing, Doug Werner (Tracks Publishing, 1999).

Surf's Up: The Girl's Guide to Surfing, Louise Southerden (Ballantine Books, 2005).

Therapeutic Landscapes: An Evidence-Based Approach to Designing Healing Gardens and Restorative Outdoor Spaces, Clare Cooper Marcus and Naomi A. Sachs (Wiley, 2013).

This Book Was a Tree: Ideas, Adventures, and Inspiration for Rediscovering the Natural World, Marcie Chambers Cuff (Perigee Trade, 2014).

Thunder Tree: Lessons from an Urban Wildland, Robert Michael Pyle (Oregon State University Press, 2011).

Tina Vindum's Outdoor Fitness: Step Out of the Gym and Into the BEST Shape of Your Life, Tina Vindum (Globe Pequot Press, 2009).

Tom Brown's Field Guide to the Forgotten Wilderness, Tom Brown (Berkley, 1987).

Tracking and the Art of Seeing: How to Read Animal Tracks and Sign, Paul Rezendes (Collins, 1999).

Treehouses and Playhouses You Can Build, David and Jeanie Stiles (Gibbs Smith, 2006).

Treehouses You Can Actually Build: A Weekend Project Book, Jeanie Trusty Stiles and David Stiles (Houghton Mifflin Company, 1998).

Unbored: The Essential Field Guide to Serious Fun, Elizabeth Foy Larsen and Joshua Glenn (Bloomsbury USA, 2012).

Unplugged Play, Bobbi Conner (Workman, 2007).

A Walk in the Woods: Rediscovering America on the Appalachian Trail, Bill Bryson (Broadway Books, 1999).

Walking Nature Home: A Life's Journey, Susan J. Tweit (University of Texas Press, 2009).

What the Robin Knows: How Birds Reveal the Secrets of the Natural World, Jon Young (Mariner Books, 2013).

Whitewater Rafting: The Essential Guide to Equipment and Techniques, Graeme Addison (Stackpole Books, 2001).

Whitewater Safety and Rescue: Essential Knowledge for Canoeists, Kayakers, and Raft Guides, Franco Ferrero (Falcon Guides, 2009.

Wild: From Lost to Found on the Pacific Crest Trail, Cheryl Strayed (Vintage Books, 2013).

Your Brain on Nature: The Science of Nature's Influence on Your Health, Happiness and Vitality, Eva M. Selhub and Alan C. Logan (Collins, 2013).

Your First Aquarium, Jay F. Hemdal (TFH Publications, Inc., 2013).

Your Natural Home: The Complete Sourcebook and Design Manual for Creating a Healthy, Beautiful and Environmentally Sensitive Home, Janet Marinelli and Paul Bierman-Lytle (Little, Brown and Co., 1995).

Notes

Introduction

xiv— *Time spent in nature may also improve*—C-D Wu, E. McNeely, J. G. Cedeño-Laurent, W-C Pan, G. Adamkiewicz, et al. (2014), Linking Student Performance in Massachusetts Elementary Schools with the "Greenness" of School Surroundings Using Remote Sensing, PLoS ONE 9(10): e108548. doi:10.1371/journal .pone.0108548.

1. The Gift of Memory

4— *Since the 1960s, child development research has yielded"*—Martha Erickson, "Shared Nature Experience as a Pathway to Strong Family Bonds," Children and Nature Network Leadership Writing Series. http://www.childrenandnature.org/wp-content /uploads/2015/04/LWS_Vol1_01.pdf.

4— *Studies show that adults receive many of the same benefits*—J. Davis, "Psychological Benefits of Nature Experiences: An Outline of Research and Theory," Naropa University, 2004.

7— *Research shows that when children play in natural play spaces*— "Outdoor Kindergartens Are Better at Stimulating Children's Creativity Than Indoor Schools," *Copenhagen Post*, October 10, 2006.

9— *Air and light pollution prevent two-thirds of the U.S.*—P. Cinzano, F. Falchi, and C. Elvidge, "The First World Atlas of the Artificial Night Sky Brightness," Monthly Notices of the Royal Astronomical Society, v. 328 (2001): 689.

2. Ways of Knowing the World

24— *Scientists who study human perception*— "How many senses does a human being have?," HowStuffWorks.com, http://science .howstuffworks.com/life/question242.htm.

26— *"If you pay rapt attention to one thing, it will dull your senses"*—Rick Curtis, "Outdoor Action Guide to Nature Observation & Stalking," 1999 Outdoor Action Program, Princeton University, http://www .princeton.edu/~oa/nature/naturobs.shtml.

27 — *The researchers found that not only are humans capable of* —
J. Porter, B. Craven, R. M. Khan, S. J. Chang, I. Kang,
B. Judkewitz, and J. Volpe, "Mechanisms of Scent-Tracking in
Humans," *Nature Neuroscience* 10, 27–29 (2007).

28 — *In 2009, researchers at Madrid's University of Alcalá de Henares* —
Juan Antonio Martínez Rojas, Jesús Alpuente Hermosilla, Pablo
Luis López Espí, and Rocío Sánchez Montero, "Physical Analysis
of Several Organic Signals for Human Echolocation: Oral Vacuum
Pulses," Acta Acustica united with Acustica 95 (2) (2009):
325–30, http://www.eurekalert.org/pub_releases/2009-06/f-sf
-ssd063009.php.

31 — *A British study in 1980 suggested that* — R. R. Baker, "Goal
Orientation by Blindfolded Humans after Long-distance
Displacement: Possible Involvement of a Magnetic Sense," *Science,*
31; 210(4469) (1980): 555–7.

31 — *Another recent theory holds that humans have so-called "grid
cells"* — Joshua Jacobs, Christoph T. Weidemann, Jonathan
F. Miller, Alec Solway, John F. Burke, Xue-Xin Wei, et al., "Direct
Recordings of Grid-like Neuronal Activity in Human Spatial
Navigation," *Nature Neuroscience,* 16 (2013): 1188–90.

32 — *Recent research suggests that the more we use GPS* — Lin Edwards,
"Study Suggests Reliance on GPS May Reduce Hippocampus
Function As We Age" (November 18, 2010), http://phys.org
/news/2010-11-reliance-gps-hippocampus-function-age.html.

35 — *Research suggests that people who get outdoors* — "What Is
Mindfulness?," The Greater Good, http://greatergood.berkeley
.edu/topic/mindfulness/definition.

47 — *A growing body of research shows that* — Wesley C. Clapp, Michael
T. Rubens, Jasdeep Sabharwal, and Adam Gazzaley, "Deficit in
Switching between Functional Brain Networks Underlies the
Impact of Multitasking on Working Memory in Older Adults,"
Proceedings of the National Academy of Sciences, USA 108, no. 17
(2011): 7212–17.

47 — *In the 1970s, environmental psychologists* — Rachel Kaplan and
Stephen Kaplan, *The Experience of Nature: A Psychological
Perspective.* New York: Cambridge University Press, 1989.

Stephen Kaplan, "The Restorative Benefits of Nature: Toward an Integrative Framework," *Journal of Environmental Psychology* 15 (1995): 169–82.

47—*Meaningful contact with nature can also*—Marc G. Berman, John Jonides, and Stephen Kaplan, "The Cognitive Benefits of Interacting with Nature," *Psychological Science* 19, no. 12 (2008): 1207–12.

49—*A Danish study found that outdoor kindergartens*—Bent Vigsø and Vita Nielsen, "Children and Outdoors," CDE Western Press, 2006. Reported in "Nature Makes Children Creative," *Copenhagen Post Online*, October 18, 2006.

49—*The University of Kansas concluded that young people*—R. A. Atchley, D. L. Strayer, and P. Atchley (2012), Creativity in the Wild: Improving Creative Reasoning through Immersion in Natural Settings, PLoS ONE 7(12): e51474. doi:10.1371/journal.pone.0051474.

65—*Researchers have shown that children who play in natural spaces*—"Outdoor Kindergartens Are Better at Stimulating Children's Creativity Than Indoor Schools," *Copenhagen Post*, October 10, 2006.

3. The Nature-Rich Home and Garden

73—*Research suggests that children strengthen their immune*—C. A. Lowry, J. H. Hollis, A. de Vries, B. Pan, L. R. Brunet, et al., "Identification of an Immune-responsive Mesolimbocortical Serotonergic System: Potential Role in Regulation of Emotional Behavior," *Neuroscience*, 146(2) (2007): 756–72.

79—*And keep cats indoors as much as possible*—"'KittyCam' Reveals High Levels of Wildlife Being Killed by Outdoor Cats," American Bird Conservancy, *National Geographic Society* (Aug. 2012), http://www.abcbirds.org/article/kittycam-reveals-high-levels-of-wildlife-being-killed-by-outdoor-cats/.

86—*In Delaware, 40 percent of all native plant species*—M. L. Rosenzweig, "Loss of speciation rate will impoverish future diversity," Proceedings of the National Academy of Sciences, USA 98 (2001): 5404–10.

87 — *Studies show that biophilic design* — R. S. Ulrich, "Biophilia, Biophobia, and Natural Landscapes," in S. A. Kellert and E. O. Wilson, eds., *The Biophilia Hypothesis*, 74–137. Washington, DC: Island Press/Shearwater.

88 — *A study conducted at a Swedish university hospital* — R. S. Ulrich and O. Lundén, "Effects of Nature and Abstract Pictures on Patients Recovering from Open-Heart Surgery." Paper presented at the International Congress of Behavioral Medicine, June 27–30, 1990, Uppsala, Sweden.

90 — *Across North America every year* — Bird Conservation Network, http://www.bcnbirds.org/window.html.

4. Nurturing Natural Resilience

110 — *Also, many grandparents* — Gretchen Livingston and Kim Parker, "Since the Start of the Great Recession, More Children Raised by Grandparents," Pew Research Center (2010).

5. Go Wild and Wilder

125 — *Only about one in five national park visitors* — Kirk Johnson, "National Parks Try to Appeal to Minorities," *New York Times*, Sept. 5, 2013, www.nytimes.com/2013/09/06/us/national-parks -try-to-appeal-to-minorities.html.

130 — *"Fewer than half of all kids"* — Centers for Disease Control and Prevention, State Indicator Report on Physical Activity, 2014. Atlanta, GA: U.S. Department of Health and Human Services, 2014.

130 — *National Parks Director Jon Jarvis* — Marc G. Berman, John Jonides, and Stephen Kaplan, "The Cognitive Benefits of Interacting with Nature," *Psychological Science* 19, no. 12 (2008): 1207–12.

135 — *The Ocean Discovery Institute in San Diego found that 90 percent* — https://orionmagazine.org/article/leave-no-child-inside/.

6. Grow Outside: The Nature Prescription

155 — *In July 2012, the* Lancet — I. M. Lee, E. J. Shiroma, F. Lobelo, P. Puska, S. N. Blair, P. T. Katzmarzyk, et al., "Effect of Physical Inactivity on Major Non-communicable Diseases Worldwide: An

Analysis of Burden of Disease and Life Expectancy," *The Lancet*, 2012; 380: 219–29, doi:10.1016/S0140-6736(12)61031-9.

157—*Comparison between people exercising on indoor treadmills*— Valerie F. Gladwell, Daniel K. Brown, Carly Wood, Gavin R. Sandercock, Jo L. Barton, "The Great Outdoors: How a Green Exercise Environment Can Benefit All," *Extrem Physiol Med*. 2013; 2: 3. Published online January 3, 2013. doi:10.1186/2046-7648-2-3.

157—*Some studies of aging suggest*—K. Day, D. Carreon, and C. Stump, "The Therapeutic Design of Environments for People with Dementia: A Review of the Empirical Research," *Gerontologist* 40, no. 4 (2000): 397–416.

158—*Studies show that experiencing nature together*—Studies include: K. Peters, B. Elands, and A. Buijs, "Social Interactions in Urban Parks: Stimulating Social Cohesion?" *Urban Forestry & Urban Greening* 9, 2 (2009): 93–100.

160—*In 2010, researchers*—Jo Barton and Jules Pretty, "What is the Best Dose of Nature and Green Exercise for Improving Mental Health? A Multi-Study Analysis," *Environmental Science and Technology* 44, no. 10 (2010): 3947–55.

161—*Researchers in Sweden have found*—M. Bodin and T. Hartig, "Does the Outdoor Environment Matter for Psychological Restoration Gained through Running?" *Psychology of Sport and Exercise*, 4 (2003): 141–53.

162—*Researchers at the University of Illinois suggest*—A. Faber Taylor and F. E. Kuo, "Could Exposure to Everyday Green Spaces Help Treat ADHD? Evidence from Children's Play Settings," *Applied Psychology: Health and Well-Being* 3 (2011): 281–303, doi:10.1111/j.1758-0854.2011.01052.x.

162—*Pennsylvania researchers have found*—See R. S. Ulrich and R. F. Simons, "Recovery from Stress During Exposure to Everyday Outdoor Environments," in *Proceedings of the Seventeenth Annual Meetings of the Environmental Design Research Association* (Washington, DC: EDRA, 1986): 115–22; J. A. Wise and E. Rosenberg, "The Effects of Interior Treatments on Performance Stress in Three Types of Mental Tasks," *CIFR*

Technical Report No. 002–02 (1988), Ground Valley State University, Grand Rapids, MI; R. S. Ulrich, "View through a Window May Influence Recovery from Surgery," *Science* 224 (1984): 420–21.

176 — *One study found trees planted on the south or west side* — G. H. Donovan and D. T. Butry, "The Value of Shade: Estimating the Effect of Urban Trees on Summertime Electricity Use," *Energy and Buildings*, June 2009, 662–68, doi:10.1016/j.enbuild .2009.01.002.

183 — *In the United States and Europe, the rate of nearsightedness among young adults* — Elie Dolgin, "The Myopia Boom," *Nature News*, 519, 276–78 (March 19, 2015). doi:10.1038/519276a.

7. The School of Nature

189 — *"Clearly, the promise of nature kindergarten made"* —http://www .timescolonist.com/opinion/op-ed/comment-we-need-to-think -beyond-nature-kindergarten-1.1733985.

190 — *One recent study, from Spain* — Payam Dadvand, Mark J. Nieuwenhuijsen, Mikel Esnaola, Joan Forns, Xavier Basagaña, Mar Alvarez-Pedrerol, Ioar Rivas, Mónica López-Vicente, Montserrat De Castro Pascual, Jason Su, Michael Jerrett, Xavier Querol, and Jordi Sunyer, "Green Spaces and Cognitive Development in Primary Schoolchildren," Proceedings of the National Academy of Sciences, USA 112 (2015): 7937–42.

190 — *A six-year study of 905 public* — *"Even after controlling for factors* — C-D Wu, E. McNeely, J. G. Cedeño-Laurent, W-C Pan, G. Adamkiewicz, et al. (2014) "Linking Student Performance in Massachusetts Elementary Schools with the 'Greenness' of School Surroundings Using Remote Sensing," PLoS ONE 9(10): e108548. doi:10.1371/journal.pone.0108548.

190 — *Similarly, preliminary results from a yet-to-be-published* — Frances E. Kuo, Landscape and Human Health Laboratory, University of Illinois at Urbana-Champaign, from personal correspondence. Karen A. Tuddenham, "Fostering Child Cognitive Development through Access to Green Space," Yale School of Forestry & Environmental Studies, http://environment.yale.edu/publication -series/documents/downloads/a-g/Berkley-2013-Section-3.pdf.

191 — *Research from the UK's John Innes Centre* — "How Roots Know Where to Grow," Live Science (2008), http://www.livescience .com/2331-roots-grow.html.

201 — *Canadian researchers report that teachers* — Anne C. Bell and Janet E. Dyment, "Grounds for Action: Promoting Physical Activity through School Ground Greening in Canada," Evergreen, 2006.

203 — *In 2010, two Oregon State University researchers* — John H. Falk and Lynn D. Dierking, "The 95 Percent Solution," *American Scientist* 98, no. 6. (2010), 486, doi:10.1511/2010.87.486.

8. The Nature-Rich Community

213 — *Research suggests that when we interact with animals* — Andrea Beetz, Kerstin Uvnäs-Moberg, Henri Julius, Kurt Kotrschal, "Psychosocial and Psychophysiological Effects of Human-Animal Interactions: The Possible Role of Oxytocin," *Frontiers in Psychology* 3 (2012): 234.

213 — *In fact, people who spend time in more natural environments* — "Nature Makes Us More Caring, Study Says," University of Rochester News, September 30, 2009.

213 — *And new studies indicate that the urban parks* — Paul A. Sandifer, Ariana E. Sutton-Grier, Bethney P. Ward, "Exploring Connections among Nature, Biodiversity, Ecosystem Services, and Human Health and Well-being: Opportunities to Enhance Health and Biodiversity Conservation," *Ecosystem Services* 12 (2014): 1–15, http://www.sciencedirect.com/science/article/pii /S2212041614001648.

214 — *Some research shows that, given the right* — F. E. Kuo and W. C. Sullivan, "Aggression and Violence in the Inner City: Impacts of Environment via Mental Fatigue," *Environment & Behavior* 33, no. 4 (2001): 543–71.

214 — *Natural playgrounds encourage more* — Karen Malone and Paul Tranter, "Children's Environmental Learning and the Use, Design and Management of Schoolgrounds," *Children, Youth and Environments* 13, no. 2 (2003).

214 — *As of 2008, for the first time in human history* — "Urbanization," United Nations Population Fund (2007), http://www.unfpa.org /urbanization.

214—*On April 23, 2015, a prestigious international group*—L. von
Hertzen, B. Beutler, J. Bienenstock, et al., "Helsinki Alert of
Biodiversity and Health," *The Annals of Medicine* (Informa
Healthcare) May 23, 2015: 218–25.

216—*Studies of workplaces created*—Among the studies of workplaces:
Vivian Loftness, as quoted in Richard Louv, *San Diego
Union-Tribune* column, July 18, 2006. David Steinman, "The
Architecture of Illness: Millions of Workers Are 'Sick of Work,'"
www.environmentalhealth.ca/fall93sick.html. Paul Hawken,
Amory Lovins, and L. Hunter Lovins, *Natural Capitalism:
Creating the Next Industrial Revolution* (New York: Back Bay
Books, 2008), 88. Kim Severson, "The Rise of Company Gardens,"
New York Times, May 11, 2010. "A Conversation with E. O.
Wilson," PBS *Nova*, April 1, 2008. Kathleen L. Wolf, "Trees Mean
Business: City Trees and the Retail Streetscape," *Main Street
News*, August 2009, 3–4.

219—*Exercise appears to have better results*—J. Pretty, J. Peacock,
M. Sellens, and M. Griffin, "The Mental and Physical Health
Outcomes of Green Exercise," *International Journal of
Environmental Health Research* 15, no. 5 (205): 319–37.

How to Get Involved in the New Nature Movement

No book can contain the full wealth of possible actions and resources useful to parents, teachers, health care providers, and other professionals, policy makers, and community organizers. To learn about additional opportunities and for an expanded list of recommended books and publications, see *Last Child in the Woods* and *The Nature Principle*, as well as the resources at RichardLouv.com. To help build the broader movement in your community, profession, or the nation, and for more information about research and how to get personally involved, please visit the Children & Nature Network at ChildrenandNature.org.

About Richard Louv

RICHARD LOUV is the author of eight books about family, nature, and community, most recently *The Nature Principle* and *Last Child in the Woods*, which have been translated into fifteen languages and published in twenty countries. He has written for the *New York Times*, the *Times of London, Orion Magazine, Parents Magazine*, and many other publications. From 1983 to 2006, he was a columnist for the *San Diego Union-Tribune*. In 2008, he was awarded the Audubon Medal; past recipients have included Rachel Carson, E. O. Wilson, and Jimmy Carter. He is the cofounder and chairman emeritus of the Children & Nature Network, and is currently working on a book about the future relationship between humans and other animals. Married to Kathy Frederick Louv, he is the father of two young men, Jason and Matthew. He would rather fish than write.

Richard Louv may be reached by e-mail at rlouv@cts.com or via the Children & Nature Network at http://www.childrenandnature.org. For more information about his work, see www.richardlouv.com.

Index